Raising Champions: A Roadmap to Success in Autism Parenting

The Ultimate Autism Parenting Guide Toolbox—Practical Techniques for Empowered Parenting From Toddlers to Teens

Brian T. Powell

© Copyright 2023 - All rights reserved.

The content contained within this book may not be reproduced, duplicated or transmitted without direct written permission from the author or the publisher.

Under no circumstances will any blame or legal responsibility be held against the publisher, or author, for any damages, reparation, or monetary loss due to the information contained within this book, either directly or indirectly.

Legal Notice:

This book is copyright protected. It is only for personal use. You cannot amend, distribute, sell, use, quote or paraphrase any part, or the content within this book, without the consent of the author or publisher.

Disclaimer Notice:

Please note the information contained within this document is for educational and entertainment purposes only. All effort has been executed to present accurate, up to date, reliable, complete information. No warranties of any kind are declared or implied. Readers acknowledge that the author is not engaged in the rendering of legal, financial, medical or professional advice. The content within this book has been derived from various sources. Please consult a licensed professional before attempting any techniques outlined in this book.

By reading this document, the reader agrees that under no circumstances is the author responsible for any losses, direct or indirect, that are incurred as a result of the use of the information contained within this document, including, but not limited to, errors, omissions, or inaccuracies.

Table of Contents

Introduction

When my son was diagnosed with both autism spectrum disorder (ASD) and attention-deficit/hyperactivity disorder (ADHD) when he was four years old, the first thing that I felt was fear. It wasn't fear of him, but *for* him—because I knew that both of these disorders brought with them stigmas that were hard to shake. I also felt overwhelmed by the diagnoses, realizing quickly that what I understood of the disorders came mostly from the media's portrayal and what I had heard "through the grapevine" over the years about these two disorders—most of which wasn't positive. Consulting with friends, family, and the internet left me with no more comfort, as most of that information reflected a lot of the same: that children with autism were difficult to parent, that they struggled with schooling and social interactions, and that they often never ended up being able to succeed on their own.

In desperation, I reached back out to my son's primary care physician, the doctor who had diagnosed him, and asked if there was anything he could tell me that might be positive in light of this news. He quickly connected me with several other families that had recently received diagnoses—both of ADHD and of ASD–some separately and some combined just like my own child. I started attending these groups and quickly gained access to resources I hadn't previously known to look for. I learned who was good to talk to and who wasn't so good, and I grew to have a circle of trusted friends and professionals that I began to trust when it came to my son's disorders.

Those first support groups, though, were just a starting point for me. Knowing that there were probably so many other parents who felt like I had when my son was diagnosed—and knowing that my son was also most likely scared and lonely in his own way—I knew that it was important for me to grasp what was going on and to provide my son with the support and the encouragement that he needed specifically to be able to succeed and thrive under the guise of these new diagnoses. With this new goal in mind, I began researching with a newfound vigor, using what I'd heard from the support groups to weed out the reliable and unreliable sources. I was able to find a plethora of new information with this perspective. In no time, I was able to begin sharing what I had learned with other families just coming into their own diagnoses with their children, specifically in regard to their children's ADHD. I consulted with doctors about all the new ways to best manage symptoms, talked with therapists and aids to see how they recommended engaging with certain behaviors and consulted other parents of neurodivergent children about their own experiences so I could best tailor my knowledge to my own son.

This seemed to push us back into the positive side of things. I won't pretend that my wife and I didn't worry, and I won't say that every day was easy, but with the information I'd learned, we were able to get a handle on my son's ADHD symptoms and implement a structure that began to work for us. We learned to cope well with my son's ADHD, picking up tricks and techniques along the way that would help us to understand and balance his needs when his brain got in the way of our communication.

I also knew, though, that a separate part of him struggled due to the intricate way that autism and ADHD contrasted each other. Understanding that his ASD needed a different criteria of aid, I set back out in search of tools to help him navigate his environment and tips for me to encourage him along. I started at the same place, back in those community groups, to see what struggles specifically some other parents were running into. From there, I started to ask doctors and researchers who specifically dealt with my son's disorder, trying to get as much of a grasp on how it might affect him as I could without having the disorder myself. I compiled this knowledge into notebooks and binders that were mostly illegible to anyone but myself—but it helped me and my wife understand my son in a way that kept him happy, healthy, and understood.

One of the most important things that I learned on this journey of discovery was that I couldn't ignore either diagnosis in favor of "bettering" the other. While the first book focused on his ADHD and this one will focus on his ASD, I need to make it known that in many cases, a combination of techniques were used to help my son balance his struggles throughout the day. When his ADHD made it hard for him to sit still, but his ASD made him want to retreat into himself for some much-needed time to regroup and destress, it was clear that his disorders were constantly at war with one another. At times, I will mention my son's ADHD, but I will, for the purposes of *Raising Champions: A Roadmap to Success in Autism Parenting,* focus on encouraging and empowering you to help your child with autism as they navigate a world that was not structured for them to be able to succeed in with ease.

As is the case with myself, I'm sure that hearing an autism spectrum disorder diagnosis attached to your child—no matter at what age it came at—was jarring and a little bit frightening. The perceptions about those with autism—that they're unloving, violent, and generally unable to thrive on their own—can make it seem like a disorder destined to drive your child into the ground. As explained in Chapter 1, however, these notions about ASD are wholeheartedly untrue. Many children with autism are affectionate, compassionate, and learn to live just as well on their own as their neurotypical peers. They may need more time to come to these conclusions and may need additional aid to reach their end goals, but there is very little standing in their way. For those children who never end up being able to live on their own, there is nothing about their diagnosis that will condemn them to a life less fulfilling than anyone else's.

The purpose of *Raising Champions* is to help guide you on a path that encourages just that. Through a thorough explanation of what ASD is in Chapter 1 and a subsequent analysis of some of the most impactful and challenging symptoms in Chapters 2 and 3—then segues into how to best support your child, your family, and yourself in various settings throughout the remainder of the book—the intention is for you to walk away feeling confident in your child's diagnosis and prepared for whatever is to come. I won't lie to you (or to myself) by saying that I have all the answers, but having spent years with my own son, interacting with families going through similar situations as me, and working with experts who are intricately familiar with his disorder, be they doctors, psychologists, or researchers, the intention is that this book may provide you a stepping stone in understanding where to go next now that your child has been diagnosed.

Hearing that your child is autistic can be scary, there's no avoiding that, but preparing yourself and your child for what that means and how to cope with their symptoms and experiences is the best way to take what the disorder brings you and remove the fear from the situation. It starts with understanding exactly what your child has just been diagnosed with.

Chapter 1:

Understanding ASD

ASD can be a confusing diagnosis to have dropped on you, as there is a lot of stigma and misunderstanding that comes along with it. A big step in the right direction when it comes to understanding how you can best help your child is to first get a grasp on the truth about what autism is and how it affects each person diagnosed. Once a strong understanding of the disorder is fostered, that knowledge can be taken and applied to your child's unique case so that you can help them grow and thrive within their own limitations and capabilities without them being pigeonholed by their diagnosis and challenges—or by a system built in complete disregard to their needs.

What Is Autism Spectrum Disorder (ASD)?

Characters with ASD are often portrayed in the media as either abrasive and rude or so oblivious to those around them that they're usually made to be the butt of most of their friends' jokes. Think of Sheldon from *The Big Bang Theory* as an example of this. Though it's often joked in the show that he's "been tested" and was never diagnosed with anything, many people in the autistic community agree that he's coded as someone with ASD—and that he's a prime example of the caricature that their disorder is often made out to be in media. Though ASD does often present with difficulties in social cues and communication, resulting in inadvertent bluntness or a lack of social awareness at times, the way that these traits come across through these characters is often exaggerated and leads to those with autism being written off. Don't get me wrong: I love the sitcom as much as the next person, but it's characters like these that can cause issues with the perception of these disorders, which is challenging for someone who watches my son deal with this disorder every day.

In truth, autism spectrum disorder (ASD) is a complex neurodevelopmental disorder that presents with difficulties in communication and strict adherence to certain routines, rituals, and behaviors—all of which Sheldon does have—that leads to extended difficulties with day-to-day tasks and more challenges with completing the same responsibilities that their neurotypical counterparts may engage in—something that isn't expressed compassionately throughout *Big Bang* (National Institute of Mental Health [NIMH], 2023). *Neurotypical* simply means a person has no disorders or differences in their brain structure or development. Alternatively, someone with a neurodevelopmental disorder such as autism or ADHD is often referred to as *neurodivergent*, as the way their brain is built or functions varies from what is accepted as "typical." ASD is usually caught early in development, as children with the disorder often struggle with meeting the same milestones as their neurotypical peers such as responding to their names, expressing emotions, or interacting with those around them in general, even from infancy (Centers for Disease Control and Prevention [CDC], 2023). Once diagnosed, ASD is something that a person will have for life, though the degree of their symptoms—and the actual symptoms that they experience—may change over the course of their life (American Psychiatric Association [APA], n.d.).

Autism used to be classified as four different disorders in the *Diagnostic and Statistical Manual of Mental Disorders,* but in the most recent fifth edition, they reduced it to just one name—autism spectrum disorder (ASD). This spectrum is vast, and it can lead to another misconception of the idea that people with autism can be "high functioning" or "low functioning." These terms have fallen out of favor now as a better understanding of how the spectrum of autism works has emerged. Put simply, the spectrum has little to do with function and a lot to do with the impact of individual symptoms.

Let's take my son, for example. Diagnosed at four years old, one of the first things that I talked about with the doctor was my son's speech. My understanding of autism prior to his diagnosis was that all people with autism were nonverbal and struggled to communicate. My son, however, was a big talker. Though he did have some of the ASD indicators, such as ignoring his name, he still loved to come to me and talk my ear off about whatever toy he'd just gotten, what he did with his mom that day, or really anything he had the language at the time to express.

When I questioned this, the answer I received was that, for verbal communication, my son did well—but he struggled in a lot of other areas. My son has a lot of difficulty with many sensory challenges, and he often becomes overwhelmed by things that go over my head like the sounds of our refrigerator or the vacuum being turned on without warning. This exemplifies that my son is not "high" or "low" on the broad spectrum, but that he experienced certain symptoms in different ways—and those ways vary from day to day.

The same could be said of your child. They may be entirely mute, but that doesn't mean that they aren't able to understand you just fine—challenges with speaking don't correlate to challenges with comprehension. Similarly, some children may struggle with sound input when it comes to sensory sensitivities, but they may have no food aversions—meaning foods that they'll go out of their way to avoid (or get turned off to on a dime due to rules that their brain believes they need to abide by). The key is to make sure that you're paying attention to your child and taking their specific symptoms into account in order to specifically accommodate their needs. Not all children will express the disorder in the same way, but that doesn't mean that any of them are "more" or "less" autistic than the next—it just means that the challenges that they face may differ, not that they need more or less support.

Symptoms of ASD

As mentioned above, the spectrum of autism is broad. Some of those diagnosed may struggle with every symptom associated with the disorder, while others may only have a few. The child with many may not experience their symptoms as severely as the child with the few, however, so it's important not to compare experiences. That being said, there are many symptoms that are characteristic of autism. Some of these will be talked about in detail in future chapters, but including a comprehensive list here felt important to make sure that a full explanation of the disorder was being provided upfront.

Communication

For starters, many people with ASD struggle with communication the same way that many characters in books or TV shows do. Be it with verbal communication, social cues, nonverbal communication such as body language or tonal shifts, or even interpretation and understanding of what's being said to them, many people with autism have a hard time with communication in some way, shape, or form (NIMH, 2023). They may also present with a flat affect—meaning a somewhat expressionless face—and a monotone voice, even when excited, angry, sad, or happy (NIMH, 2023). Chapter 2 will discuss the challenges of communication in more detail.

Sensory

Another major symptom of autism is struggles with sensory input. Many people with autism struggle with sensory overload, be that from auditory input, visual input, or even tactile input—sometimes even a combination of multiple of these at once (NIMH, 2023). This sensation can often be referred to as being *overstimulated* when there's too much going on at once and their system can't regulate all the inputs being thrown at them.

Think of it like the TVs we used to have before HDMI cables, which had three separate plugs—one for visual, one for audio right, and one for audio left—to be plugged into the device we wanted to use, like a DVD player (or even a VCR). In this scenario, your child is the TV receiving these inputs, and the DVD player is the world. That cord is what it is—the transmitter for all that information. A neurotypical person may be able to handle all three plugs at once. With all systems go, they can take in the images and the sound and sort out where everything needs to go all at once, no questions asked.

For someone with ASD, however, something in that TV glitches, and the ability to take in all those inputs all at once is short-circuited. Their audio may get too loud on one side at times or too soft. The color may go negative, then positive, then only red and green. Sometimes the image may cut out entirely. The only way for it to function effectively again is to either twist one of the plugs for a temporary fix—such as masking—or to unplug the wire that's causing the issue—like wearing sound-canceling headphones to help bring everything back to baseline.

When overstimulation like this occurs, those with ASD may stim to try to regulate themselves, remove themselves from the situation, or melt or shut down. These meltdowns and shutdowns are usually recognizable, as the child may start to lash out, cry, or scream due to the overstimulation—meltdowns—or they may disengage from the situation at hand entirely—shutdowns. There will be a little bit more on this in Chapter 3.

Routine and Structure

Autism is also known for the routines and structure that it demands of those diagnosed with it. Many people understood this from what was formerly known as Asperger's syndrome, where certain people only ate certain foods on certain days, followed certain schedules throughout those days, and maybe even had certain clothes for those certain days as well. With Asperger's now being understood as part of the autism spectrum, many others being diagnosed are noticing these habits in themselves as well. There are classic representations of these desires, such as wanting their days to unfold in a specific way, for events to occur in a particular sequence, or for tasks or habits to be carried out in a predetermined way. If these routines aren't followed, it can cause discomfort, unease, or even the same meltdowns or shutdowns as above. This is why sudden changes in plans often aren't something that people with autism take well.

This desire for structure also reveals itself in other, similar ways. They may have foods they consider to be "safe," such as meals they limit themselves to eating at given restaurants because they're trusted. They may also only have specific activities that they like to participate in when going out with family or friends because those places are familiar and understood to them. Having these safe places and foods allows them to maintain control over the situations and environments that they find themselves in so they can maintain a certain amount of understanding, regulation, and calm during whatever it is they need to do.

Emotional Disconnection

It is also a common misconception that those with autism are cold. Because they have a flat affect or often misunderstand emotional cues, they often do not seem properly engaged with their own emotions or with the emotions of those around them. This leads people to believe that they're uncaring or robot-like. The truth is that many people with autism struggle with alexithymia—which is just a scientific word for having difficulty with identifying their own emotions, expressing them, or commiserating with the emotions of those around them (Wilkinson, 2017). It's estimated that upwards of 85% of people with autism have some involvement of alexithymia with their diagnosis (Wilkinson, 2017). It is theorized that autism and alexithymia are separate conditions, as alexithymia can occur in the general population and alongside other conditions and disorders (Wilkinson, 2017), but this doesn't change the fact that those with autism are not cold on purpose—they just struggle with emotions because of the disorder they have.

Literal Thinking

Another common symptom linked to autism that many people tend to claim to understand is literal thinking. With ASD, many people often struggle with figurative language such as metaphors and sarcasm. They may also struggle with tone shifts—such as when one person says something but their tone suggests another—or when people aren't direct about what they're trying to say. These forms of communication often make little sense to them, and they'll end up taking whatever is being said literally—which can end up causing a lot of sticky situations. Of course, in media, this often gets portrayed as being funny or comical in some sense, but in actuality, this can lead to a lot of humorless situations where one or more people are being left out or getting their feelings hurt.

This way of thinking, where statements are taken at face value, also means that many people with autism will follow rules that are given to them to a T. Whether this be verbal instruction, written instruction, or otherwise, the need to fulfill those requirements will take the forefront of their mind because that's what they were told to do—even if someone tells them there is a more efficient way to do it.

Causes of ASD

There is a lot of evidence to support the idea that ASD is caused by genetic mutations, though very little is still known about the disorder as a whole and many research studies are still being conducted to help get a better understanding of how and why autism occurs (Eunice Kennedy Shriver National Institute of Child Health and Human Development, 2017). Some factors may lead to a higher risk of a person being born with autism, such as having a sibling or parent who's already been diagnosed with autism, having a secondary genetic or chromosomal condition, birth complications, or older parents (CDC, 2022-c).

How Is ASD Diagnosed?

There is no one specific test that confirms if a person has autism. Even with implications of a genetic component, there are so many different genes suspected to be involved and so many different combinations that those mutations could factor in that there is ultimately no test to be run to confirm if a person does in fact have autism.

Instead, diagnosis generally comes from observation of the child over the course of their early development. Parents are encouraged to monitor a child's developmental milestones through the first three years of their life and to make note of any delayed markers or missed steps up to 30 months. Doctors will also check in at measured intervals—usually at 9, 18, and 30 months—to make sure that children are developing on par with the rest of their peers. It's recommended as well that all children are screened for ASD symptoms at 18 months and again at 30 months (CDC, 2022-b).

These screenings usually focus on a child's language skills, motor skills, and thinking skills in addition to their general behavior and emotional state. If a child is suspected of having autism, interviews will be conducted with the parents or primary caregivers, the professionals in the child's life such as their school teachers, and even the child if they are old enough or have the social skills to participate. All of this monitoring and screening is based on the standard measures detailed out in the *Diagnostic and Statistical Manual of Mental Disorders (DSM-V).* Most of these diagnoses can be made within the first three years of life, though in more difficult cases, some doctors may opt to delay while they continue to observe. This can occur in certain instances when a child may develop at a normal rate in their earlier years and then suddenly regress, which does occur with many children who have autism.

Diagnostic ratios seem to favor boys currently, though there is some evidence to support that skew comes from criteria that favored a male presentation of the disorder. As more understanding comes to light with how the disorder presents and is experienced in girls and women, the gap between genders closes.

Co-Occurring Disorders

As with many disorders that are this complex, autism does have the opportunity to appear alongside a plethora of other disorders. Some of these may be physical, which would be considered *comorbid* disorders. Many, however, are mental disorders or illnesses, which are instead referred to as *co-occurring.* Both come with their own sets of complications, but for the purposes of this book, the focus will remain on the latter.

Seizures

As many as one out of every four children diagnosed with autism will experience seizures to some degree throughout their lives (Autism Empowerment, n.d.). Some may struggle with absent seizures or episodes where it seems that they may be stuck staring but are completely unresponsive to external stimuli, while others may struggle with more classically understood seizures that are characterized by convulsions and passing out. Electroencephalograms (EEGs) can help to confirm the presence of seizures in most cases, though in some instances, children with autism express abnormal EEGs as their base, so it can still be hard to tell (Autism Empowerment, n.d.).

Fragile X Syndrome

Children with fragile X syndrome are already at a higher risk of also being diagnosed with autism, but the correlation goes both ways. Fragile X is caused by a mutation in the X chromosome and has a range of symptoms that can present from mild to severe (Autism Empowerment, n.d.). In many cases, these symptoms can appear to be very similar to ASD and may even be confused with the disorder, but the truth is that they often exist in tandem with one another rather than in place of one another. Roughly 1 out of every 25 children who has autism also has the mutation for fragile X, even if the secondary disorder does not present as severely (Autism Empowerment, n.d.).

ADHD

Attention-deficit/hyperactivity disorder (ADHD) is one of the most commonly co-diagnosed disorders when it comes to autism, presenting in about 71% of children with autism (Mosner, et. al., 2019). ADHD is another neurodevelopmental disorder that is characterized by difficulties with self-regulation—which is usually better understood as difficulty with impulse control, focusing, and hyperactivity. It can come in direct contrast to many children who have autism and like structure, rules, and regiments, which can cause additional conflict and difficulty for the child that's been diagnosed.

Savant Syndrome

It's a common faux pas made that all children with autism spectrum disorder are considered to be savants. The fact of the matter is that while savant syndrome occurs at a much higher rate among those with ASD—occurring in 1 out of every 10 people with autism or up to 28% according to some sources (SSM Health, n.d., Autistica, 2018)—it is still nowhere close enough to being considered all of them. Savant syndrome, however, is still worth mentioning because of the frequency at which it does occur. There are three specific types of savant syndrome that are usually identified:

- "splinter" savants, in which the skills allow for acute memorization of facts, number sequences, sounds, or preoccupations with certain topics to the point of seeming to understand everything about it;

- "talented" savants, in which a person's skills are "more prominent and highly honed" in areas of art, music, or mathematics to the point that they are usually held in high regard "despite their overall handicap"; and

- "prodigious" savants, in which their skills are taken to such a high level that, should it have occurred in someone without a disability, it would be considered a genius-level skill. (It feels important to note that the title of a prodigious savant is given out so rarely that fewer than 100 of these particularly skilled persons are currently named worldwide.) (SSM Health, n.d.)

Savant syndrome can occur in neurotypical people and people with different disabilities, so they are included in the information provided above; however, due to the high percentage of those with autism who are also diagnosed with savant syndrome, it was worth noting in detail here—with the caveat, again, that not all people with ASD have a savant-like talent.

Myths About ASD

Autism can be a scary diagnosis to receive because of the stigma that comes with it, but it doesn't help that it's also swimming in myths. So many people misconstrue the disorder because of what is often said about it—much of which is untrue or simply misunderstood.

Autism Is Caused by Vaccines

Perhaps the most common myth about autism that circulates is that it is caused by vaccinations. Though this theory has been widely disproven, many people still believe that vaccinating their children puts them at a higher risk of "contracting" autism. The vaccination discussion aside, it's important to understand that autism is something that a child is born with, it's not something that they can be given. It has to do with genetic makeup, not with medical input such as vaccines or medications. Since the early 2000s, many studies have been conducted that prove no correlation exists between vaccinations and autism or any of the preservatives used in the vaccinations (CDC, 2022-a).

Autism Is a Childhood Condition (That Only Affects Boys)

Another misconception about autism is that it is a childhood condition and that as the person ages, they will grow out of it. The truth of the matter is that autism is a chronic and lifelong disorder. Once diagnosed, a person will be considered autistic forever. The severity in which their disorder affects them may vary and even lessen with age, and many people with autism do go on to lead successful and fulfilling lives with minimal intervention. Even those who require lifelong aid can be successful and happy. Regardless of where they fall on the spectrum with their symptoms, there are many autistic adults. Today, there are also many people who don't receive their diagnosis until adulthood—particularly women, as the understanding of how the disorder presents in girls and women is still gaining understanding. Diagnoses in girls are also on the rise, as mentioned before, and the disparity between diagnosis in boys and diagnosis in girls is slowly narrowing.

All People With Autism Are Savants

This was mentioned in the co-occurring conditions section, but it's worth mentioning again in greater detail. It's true that about 28% of people with autism have an inexplicable talent in one way or another (Autistica, 2018) but the idea that all children with autism have a special talent is a gross overestimation. This can be attributed, again, to the media's portrayal of autism. Movies like *A Beautiful Mind*—though based on a true story—and *The Good Doctor* all show autistic people with amazing talents in their field. All over social media, too, we see autistic children who can paint skylines from memory or do complex math problems without a piece of paper. But it shouldn't be the expectation that just because your child is autistic they will have a superhuman talent. Some children with autism are perfectly average—and that's perfectly okay.

People With Autism Are Antisocial, Cold, and Unfeeling (With No Sense of Humor)

It's true that people with autism often struggle to "read the room" when it comes to emotions and tonal shifts during conversation. This lack of skill, however, often leads to the misconception that people with autism are incapable of feeling, would rather not socialize with others, and may even not be funny because they often miss the jokes flying back and forth between their friends. The truth of it is actually that much of what happens in these situations—emotional exchanges, sarcastic conversations, and social gatherings in general—happens through nonverbal communication, such as body language, facial expressions, hand gestures, and tonal shifts—all things that people with autism often struggle to pick up on. Moreover, people with autism generally struggle to find the language that they need to express their emotions and struggle even harder to be able to commiserate on an emotional level with other people because of the need to identify those emotions, understand them, and then designate the appropriate response. So, it isn't that people with autism are cold and careless—it really is that they struggle with the information-processing part of these interactions. They struggle with the subtleties of these interactions and may come off as cold or humorless when they miss the sarcastic comment or tonal shift in a conversation. The mistakes are usually genuine, and a quick explanation often leads to an understanding of the joke and their ability to participate in the activity. In cases like these, patience and understanding is key.

People With Autism Hate Being Touched

Similarly to the above, people believe that because those with autism often move away from touches from strangers or shy away from physical contact, they completely hate being touched and are overly dramatic about it. In many of these instances, though, the person with autism is affectionate or enjoys physical touch—but just with warning, permission, and from the right people. People with autism like to understand their environment and have an awareness of the things that are going on around them. If someone were to come up behind them and touch them unexpectedly, it could set them into a panic because that was unexpected for them in an environment where they were already struggling to remain regulated. Additionally, many people with autism struggle with secondary conditions including sensory processing disorders or obsessive-compulsive disorder (OCD), so any one of these could be thrown into a downward spiral at just a casual touch. A way that this can be avoided is simply by making your presence known, asking if the touch is okay, and terminating the touch when the person seems ready for it to be done.

Autism Is Caused by Bad Parenting

As previously stated throughout the chapter, autism is caused by genetic mutations and genetic inheritance. It is also something that people are born with. There is nothing to suggest that poor parenting can cause autism or worsen it.

Autism Can Be Cured

Autism is a chronic condition, meaning that once a person is diagnosed with it, they will have it forever. Their symptoms may vary over time, improving or worsening, changing or growing as they do. They can be managed by medication, by therapy, or by time. In no way, though, can autism be cured.

ASD and Its Impact

Living with autism, no matter where one falls on the spectrum, is not an easy undertaking. With a consistent overload of sensory information, the demand for communication and processing of a world that isn't built for their needs, and a lack of understanding of their disorder, it can be hard to figure out where they fit. This can lead to major challenges in many aspects of their lives, many of which will be discussed in greater detail in the coming chapters, but all of which will be touched on here.

Social

Autism causes impairment in multiple aspects of communication, which can lead to difficulties with making and maintaining friends. Children with autism may come off as tactless or harsh because they don't have a comprehension of social conventions, leading to other children isolating them or bullying them. They may also isolate themselves because they don't understand the social landscape, as well as potentially struggle to find their place among peers as they stand out from the rest or may adapt to what's expected of them in order to fit in—something called *masking*. This entails hiding what is considered to be their autistic traits from prying eyes to appear normal. In these cases, they may experience burnout, overwhelm, fatigue, or exhaustion at higher rates than their peers because they aren't able to regulate or express themselves when needed.

Academic (and Professional)

In academic settings, children with autism may struggle because of either communication problems or a lack of understanding. Due to literal thinking, many children with autism ask for direct and clear instructions on what is expected from them in tasks and assignments. If the instructions are too vague, they may experience stress and be unable to complete the task. In school, children with autism may also still struggle with general overwhelm and communicating their needs, as these settings are streamlined for efficacy and leave little room for children to "catch up" when they need it.

Familial

In family settings, children with autism may be othered or babied, leading to a secondary type of "othering." Many children with autism are able to function independently with very little intervention, but there can be instances when parents overstep their bounds. This can lead to their child feeling different as well as to them feeling as though they're separated from the rest of their family. Other children in the family, similarly, may feel a certain level of favoritism toward their neurodivergent sibling and may act unfairly toward them. It can also occur where side comments go unnoticed by family members about the "oddness" of children with autism. This is where it becomes important to let your child come to you when they need help—if they're able to communicate these needs—or to know where the line is so that you don't overstep, but also to know where to keep your own boundaries so your own family doesn't create a place where your child may feel they need to hide and mask from even you.

To Recap

Autism spectrum disorder (ASD) is a neurodevelopmental disorder that leads to struggles in communication, difficulty with processing sensory input, and a seemingly compulsive need to follow rules and schedules. It can be a dictator over the diagnosed person's life and lead to difficulty with making and maintaining relationships. It can also cause difficulty with learning, working, or functioning in a daily capacity. Children with ASD are often miscategorized as unaffectionate, violent, or "odd," but these are often untrue. With the right amount of patience and understanding about their disorder and how their brain works, many children with autism are found to be perfectly loving and exceptionally funny in their own ways.

In the following chapters, more will be explained about how to maximize communication between yourself and your child with autism, no matter their capabilities. Behavioral issues will also be discussed in addition to learning challenges and promoting independence and emotional knowledge. Toward the end of the book, support will be offered for how to best prepare yourself as a parent for parenting a child with autism and how to best prepare your family, so no one in the support system will feel as though they're being left out.

Chapter 2:

Effective Communication Strategies

Communication is one of the key components of our everyday lives. Whether we intend to do so or not, we communicate with nearly every person we cross paths with—through our facial expressions, our body language, the tone in which we greet them if we do, and even the hand gestures we use if we don't say anything at all. For many neurotypical people, these communications are so subtle that we may not even realize that we're processing and understanding them. When a person waves you on in traffic, you raise your hand as thanks and then take your turn. That was a conversation. When something strange happens in public, you may make eye contact with a stranger and raise your eyebrows as if to say, "Did you see that?", and they may do it back in a silent, "I know, right?" As such, you essentially conversed with them without even opening your mouth. Even the quintessential awkwardness of trying to walk around someone, only to have them move to do the same so you block each other's paths again is a form of communication. Each day, we participate in these actions a dozen times and don't even think about them. Then with our friends and families, when verbal communication is involved, or when sarcasm is thrown into the mix, we may joke and laugh and talk without a second to pause and consider the *how* or the *why* of exactly what's being said. It all comes naturally, with so much ease that a second to pause isn't even necessary. We just *understand.*

For those with autism, however, these daily interactions are a constant cause of stress and strain. The more difficulty they experience with different aspects of communication processing, the more likely they are to experience stress with different aspects of these interactions as well.

Autism's Effect on Communication

For those with autism, the ease with which the above interactions come is interrupted by the person's inability to process the information in the same way that a neurotypical person might. This isn't to say that they're completely incapable of it, but just that they may need to do it in a different way, either with more time or after having a particular perspective provided to them.

Communication is understood as a type of transaction for many people. When we talk to someone, we understand that what we put into it, we'll most likely get out of it. This transaction can deal in ideas, feelings, worries, likes, dislikes, and so many other things. For those with autism, however, this transactional understanding is not part of the communication outline. The start of this difficulty comes with a general issue with understanding how one might start or continue a conversation. Think of all the times when you've been talking to someone and you didn't know what you were supposed to say. Many people with autism feel like this *all the time.*

This lack of knowing what to say comes from the way that their language skills developed as children. For many, they never developed an understanding of that transaction—and they also mean what they say because of how literally they think and deliberately they act. This often means they don't understand the need for niceties or small talk because it holds no value to them or they often don't mean the things that are being said. It isn't that they're deliberately being cold or rude—they just simply don't see the point.

Scripting

This lack of knowing what to say may lead to people with autism filling in the blanks with ready-made "scripts"—either from things they've heard others around them say or from the media that they consume. In many cases, these scripts are already constructed so that they'll have something to say no matter the situation—similar to "create your own adventure" stories. If they begin the conversation, they'll usually have answers for any one of a number of responses—a learned behavior to keep the conversation going. They may also practice certain things they want to or need to say in the mirror in order to become more comfortable with saying whatever it is that they need to.

Echolalia

Scripts can sometimes also use repeated statements that they've heard others—even the person they intend to talk to—say. The repetition of words or phrases—usually out of context or without a meaning attached to them—is known as *echolalia* (The Spectrum, 2020). People with autism may sometimes use this repetition to help fill in the gaps in their abilities to communicate, such as responding to the question they're asked with the same question as "yes" or even asking that question when they mean to ask for permission instead. With children with autism, this transposition of statements and meanings is common.

My son—like most children—really liked ice cream as a child, but because of his ADHD, we would often regulate how much he could have at a given time. We would also sometimes use it as a motivator for good behavior—his reward—and we would refer to it as such. When he completed a desired task or executed a desired behavior, we would say to him, "Here's your treat!" and give him an ice cream—sometimes a scoop, sometimes ice cream on a stick if we had it. That phrase became the question he would ask when he wanted ice cream from that point until he was in his teen years. When he wanted ice cream, he'd come up to us, and instead of asking, "Can I have some ice cream?", he'd instead say, "Here's your treat!"

Monologuing

The main struggle with verbal communication when it comes to autism is maintaining the back-and-forth of a conversation with others. Many people with autism will have language and speech skills—meaning that they will be able to talk and comprehend what's being said around them—but they may struggle, as said before, with knowing what to say and when to say it.

This may lead to children monologuing rather than dialoguing. With dialogue, just like with reading a book, two or more people are speaking—usually having a back-and-forth conversation. With monologuing, though, only one person is speaking at a particular time. Children with autism may feel more comfortable monologuing because there's no conversation to maintain; they know what they want to say and don't need to formulate responses to something else a person has said.

These monologues usually come in regard to their special interests or particular areas of interest rather than just in simple conversation, and they will leave very little breathing room for a person to cut in and say something. In less common instances, a person with autism may speak at length about anything in general without stopping, still holding a monologue, but not about any one particular subject.

Identifying Communication Challenges in Children With Autism Spectrum Disorder

Communication symptoms are usually one of the first indications that a child may need to be monitored or tested for autism spectrum disorder. It can usually be identified by watching how your child's language skills develop in their early childhood. Some of this was discussed in Chapter 1, but to reiterate here for the sake of keeping similar information together in one place, it's worth mentioning some of it again.

Not Responding to Their Name

Many children without autism will start to respond to their name being called before they've even turned a year old, acknowledging these summons with a head turn, a smile, or even going to the person who's called them if they're already able to move about on their own. For children with autism, however, this response time is delayed—if it comes at all. This does not mean that they don't comprehend the title as their name, per se, but it does indicate a disconnect. By nine months, if children are not responding to their names, it's something to keep an eye on.

Slow Language Development

All children develop language skills at different rates. Children in multilingual houses in particular may show delayed language development as they are learning to process two languages—only to later have an explosion of understanding in both languages and be able to communicate effectively in whichever languages are spoken around them with regularity. Other children still may struggle with language learning due to learning disabilities or other developmental disorders that have nothing to do with autism at all. Hence why it can sometimes be more difficult to track language development alone as a means to indicate whether a child may or may not be on the spectrum. Language development, though, is still worth mentioning because of the intricate ways in which autism likes to intertwine itself with the way that we communicate in our daily lives.

There are two main ways in which autism can make itself known through early childhood language skills. The first is simple: Your child may struggle to grasp learning how to speak and may have a limited number of words they're able to comprehend and use if they're able to use any at all. This one is common among many other disorders, however, so it can be more of a wait-and-see type of indicator rather than a cut-and-dry aid. The other way that autism can rear its head when it comes to early language development is through regression. In a lot of instances, many children with autism will hit their developmental milestones for the first 18 to 24 months of their lives—speaking with fluency or even above the predicted rate. Then suddenly, they may have a drastic backslide. They may stop learning after a certain point and only start speaking a few words again, or may even become entirely mute.

Because of the tricky nature of autism, this is not always a hard and fast rule, so it's always best to consult with your child's primary care physician and check in at all of the usual milestones and monitoring points—especially if your child is already being watched for autism.

Lack of Eye Contact

Eye contact can be a difficult part of communication for people with autism due to the stress and overstimulation that eye contact can bring along with it. In many cases, those with autism may only hold eye contact for brief periods of time if they hold it at all (Dale, 2022). Eye contact can be distracting in another sense for those with autism because they will often think more about maintaining eye contact—whether they should be maintaining it, if they've maintained it too long, if they're looking at the correct eye—rather than what the conversation is truly about. Some may even close their eyes while talking with someone so that all of their attention can be turned entirely to the conversation at hand (Dale, 2022).

Flat Affect

Those with autism also often have a flat affect, meaning that they often don't communicate their emotions on their face or even with gestures. This can start in early development and persist through to adulthood. Some children, especially girls, may learn to mirror others when expressing their emotions as part of their "masks" but they often have a hard time learning to identify and express these feelings on their own. They also may feel as though they are effectively communicating with them when they aren't.

Improving Communication With Your Child With ASD

One of the important things to remember when it comes to communicating with your child with ASD is that you aren't trying to fix or change them. Rather, your goal is to help accommodate their individual and unique way of communicating so that they can feel more comfortable with themselves while also encouraging their social skills so that they'll feel comfortable interacting in larger and less controlled settings. While there are ways to help control some of these interactions while your child is in school through 504 plans and IEPs—which will be discussed in detail in a later chapter—there are other ways in which you can help encourage your child's social skills while also supporting their unique ways of communication as well.

Speaking Clearly

Children with autism often struggle with nuance, meaning that implied language or rhetorical questions that code what you'd like for them to do will often result in confusion over what is being asked of them. Rather than leaving them wondering what you meant, leaving it up to interpretation and ambiguity, or creating a situation that results in disappointment on your end, guilt on their end, or fighting on both ends, just speak directly to your child about what you'd like for them to do. It always felt harsh at first to turn to my son and say, "Vacuum the rug, please," but when he was old enough to talk about it with us, we learned that he really appreciated this directness. It helped to make sure that the expectations were clear to him.

If you have multiple children in the house, it can be helpful also to include names in these directions. Pet names can sometimes be confusing, as well as terms of endearment, so it can be an important tool to add a direct name address to these directions that you give. If your child has a nickname that they know is specific to them or that they really enjoy, that may be the exception to the rule. Assess your own situation with your child to see how this might apply.

Entertaining Their Preferred Topics

As mentioned previously, many children with ASD tend to have topics they seem to fixate on. They can discuss these topics at length, usually in a monologue format, without getting bored or without the usual communication hiccups they tend to experience with other communication experiences or formats.

It can be beneficial to both you and your child to encourage and participate in these topics of discussion when they come up. They will encourage your child's communication skills as well as build positive bonds of support between the two of you. More than that, it can sometimes be used as a segue into other topics that will allow you to facilitate further development of their communication skills.

Augmentative and Alternative Communication (AAC)

Whether your child is verbal or nonverbal, there can still be times when verbal communication is too much for them to process at a particular point. This is where visual aids or written instructions can come in handy. Augmentative and alternative communication (AAC) encompasses the various ways that communication can be done without verbal communication: written communication, sign language and gestures, visual communication like pictures, and even electronic communication using computers as aids. These different forms of communication are usually broken down into two different types: aided and unaided AAC. Unaided AAC includes hand-based aids such as sign language, gestures or writing, while aided AAC includes anything that uses an additional tool such as those that use picture books, usually considered low aid, and those that use computer aids, which are considered high aid (The Spectrum, 2020).

Written Communication

While verbal communication is a big part of how our world operates on the day-to-day, it can also be a lot to take in all at once. For those with processing delays or issues with overwhelm and overstimulation, having instructions or information written down can be an easier way for people with autism to take that information and process it in smaller, easier-to-digest chunks. This way, they can also revisit it if something seems unclear, make themselves notes if they need something clarified, or simply work their way down the list.

Written communication doesn't just have to be about instruction or information though. Having text or email communication can be a great way to allow two-way conversation which gives the other person more time to see your answer and formulate a response. The only issue with this is that text is often toneless, so it can be even harder, in some ways, to convey how something should come across. In recent years, the online platform has come up with something called "tone tags" which allow people to tag how their written words are supposed to come across (Paavlova, 2022). Different from emojis—which are sometimes used ironically, another nonverbal communication device that goes over the heads of those with autism a lot of the time—tone tags literally tell the reader that something is sarcastic ("/s"), genuine ("/gen"), or joking ("/j") (Paavlova, 2022). Unlike when someone says "jk" ("just kidding") after saying something off-color or mean, these tags are usually regarded with more kindness and are used in a literal sense to help those who struggle with tone understand the context of what's been said.

If written communication is still something not quite in the cards, pictures can also be another really helpful way to help children get their needs met.

Visual Aids

Picture books that have images of common items such as favorite foods, favorite places, or favorite activities can be a major aid in homes where verbal communication isn't the first line of defense. These books can be given to the child to ask them to point to what they want, or they can be used by the caregiver to indicate something being asked or a task that needs to be completed.

Some families that I worked with in the community groups put their pictures on velcro so that when a task needed to be completed, they could be moved to a bigger task board for the child to see. When the task was completed it could be moved back to the book. Their child, who was nonverbal, also took advantage of this and removed the velcro squares to bring to their parents to ask for snacks or to go to the park rather than bringing the entire book with them.

Hands as Communication

Sign language is another major player when it comes to nonverbal communication—and it's not something that leaves your child limited to communication with just a handful of people. Sign language, just like any other, is a language that can be used to communicate with anyone else who also speaks it, meaning that any other people in the area that use sign language to communicate can also speak with your child. This is one of the major benefits to signing as well, as it can greatly broaden your child's social scope. Without having to use their voice, they can enhance their social skills.

If they're not to a capacity where learning a full language is possible, rudimentary signs or even signs that you or your family can understand are still effective communication tools. Gestures also work well so long as they can be understood by your child, their primary caregivers, and those who immediately interact with them.

Electronic Aids

There are also electronic speech aids that can be used in place of your child's own voice should that be something that you feel is conducive to your child and their environment. These can usually be downloaded to computers or tablets, and they work simply by typing what your child would like to say into them.

The Impacts of Poor Communication

With poor communication skills, all aspects of a person's life can be impacted. Though verbal communication specifically is not necessary for a good quality of life, having a way to interact with other people and the world around you is something that can have a great positive effect on your experiences in the environments that you frequent. Without fostering these communication skills—be they verbal, visual, or physical—your child could struggle in any of the following areas.

Social

To form close friendships, communication in some capacity is needed. Generally, friends start being friends by an initial greeting or introduction. Whether that's with a "hello," a wave, or a simple nod, some sort of communication is needed to initiate that contact. Without communication skills, your child won't know how to initiate these interactions, and they therefore may struggle to make and maintain friends. As it is, children with autism struggle with the two-way communication style, so having confidence in their own form of communication and an understanding of how communication works—even if they don't initially participate—can set them up for successful relationships in the long run.

Academic (and Professional)

Similarly, in academic settings, if a child does not understand what's expected of them in a particular setting, they might not be prepared to absorb the information put before them. Without an understanding of communication, children in academic settings may not know when to pay attention, may not learn how to pick out "the important parts" of what's being said to them, and may have an even harder time sorting through the information given to them in order to make sense of it. They may also struggle with the multiple conversations being held around them at any given point and become overwhelmed without ever being able to participate in any of them. Giving children with ASD an understanding of communication and ways to control how they engage with such things can help them here.

Familial

With family, it can be difficult because the group is usually much smaller—until the holidays when the group is much bigger and filled with people whom the child is not familiar with. In either context, there can be discomfort because there's pressure to participate in conversations they're not sure how to contribute to. They may often sit back or remove themselves entirely, finding the setting too overwhelming to be a part of. This may lead to the perception that they're rude or not loving—myths that were debunked in Chapter 1. Instead, giving children the liberty to discuss their safe topics can allow them a safe way to contribute to conversations without having to retreat and still not have to participate in the conversation in a way that would make them uncomfortable.

To Recap

Communication is one of the biggest pain points of living with ASD. Between verbal cues and nonverbal cues, as well as the demands of two-way conversation that can sometimes be unclear and difficult to maintain, there are a lot of "traps" that people with ASD are afraid to fall into. When it comes to helping your child with ASD communicate, remember that there are other ways other than verbal that they can get what they need to say across. Using their hands, using pictures, or even sending a text can be a helpful way of allowing your children to communicate without forcing them into situations that may lead to overstimulation and meltdowns. Remember, of course, that the goal is not to teach them how to communicate like their neurotypical peers, but to give them tools that they can use to participate in the conversation in the way that best benefits them.

Chapter 3:

Behavior Management and Positive Discipline

I mentioned in the Introduction that there are a lot of misconceptions regarding autism and the behavioral implications that come along with an autism diagnosis. The commonly accepted, social understanding of autism is that autistic children tend to throw tantrums and are overly violent due to their disorder. Though it was already said, it's worth mentioning again that this isn't the case. Though there is a high percentage of children who experience these bursts of anger, this does not mean that they are any more violent or aggressive than the neurotypical children they share a classroom with. More than that, if an effort is being made to understand where these behaviors are coming from and how to best interact with them, then the frequency with which they happen and the likelihood for them to continue to occur can be reduced or even eliminated.

Why Children With Autism "Misbehave"

It's a fact of life that all children misbehave. They like to push the limits of the boundaries they've been given to see where they can get to before they really get in trouble. It's not much different with children with autism. They, too, want to push their limits and see what they can get away with.

The difference with children with autism is that these "misbehaviors" are often done with a certain level of motivation behind them. Be it that they're overstimulated or that there's something they're trying to communicate but are not effectively able to, they may use less than favorable behaviors in order to get their way or communicate their displeasure in something. With communication already such an area of difficulty for many of those diagnosed, as mentioned in the last chapter, these tantrums can be effective because many parents or caregivers will do anything to make it stop—which usually means giving in to whatever it is that's being demanded.

Putting it this way makes it seem like the child with autism is doing these things intentionally, and while in some cases that may be true, that's not a blanket statement—or even true in most of the cases of poor behavior. In reality, these children don't have an effective way to communicate their needs, so they scream or cry to communicate their frustration because they've seen that done somewhere else and are mirroring it or because that's all they can think to do in their heightened state. The issue comes when that behavior is then reinforced when they get their way as the parent removes them from the unpleasant situation. Again, this doesn't mean that your child should remain somewhere that makes them uncomfortable, but the way in which they communicate their needs via these behaviors is key. This will be circled back to in a minute when the discussion turns to how to better prepare for these meltdowns and how to handle them. Here, the focus will remain on why these behaviors occur for a bit longer.

Identifying Unfavorable Behaviors

Unfavorable behaviors can be classified as anything that puts your child or others in harm's way, emotional disturbances or dysregulation when something doesn't go their way, persistent social impairment, complaints about physical ailments, or refusing to follow rules, requests, or boundaries. This can appear in the form of self-injury, aggression toward others, withdrawal from social settings, persistent headaches or stomachaches, or a blatant refusal to do chores being asked of them.

The motivation for any one of these could be to try to escape or avoid a situation that makes them uncomfortable. Be that discomfort from an internal or external source, the result is the same.

Evaluating the Meltdowns

It's also important to understand that these meltdowns, tantrums, or outbursts don't just happen out of nowhere. Generally, there's an inciting incident that sets things in motion that's then compounded by a situational obstacle that ultimately leads to the meltdown. A study done by Stephen M. Edelson regarding this thought process suggests that in each scenario where a child with autism acts out, there is usually a setting event or a preexisting condition that's already causing distress within the child and an antecedent, which is usually an activity that the child already wants to avoid (Edelson, 2022). Both of these things usually motivate a behavior that is meant as a catalyst for expressing their discomfort or getting away from the unwanted situation (Edelson, 2022). The reaction to that behavior is known as the consequence (Edelson, 2022).

For an easier-to-understand explanation, let's consider my son when he first started school. My son, thanks to both his ADHD and his ASD, is prone to headaches. He gets them pretty frequently, and we're relatively good at handling them now. But when he was small and didn't quite understand what they were or how to communicate what was happening to us, it led to a lot of sticky situations. One of the main catalysts for poor behavior, in the beginning, was when he had a headache and also had to be at school. Having not told us that his head hurt—through no fault of his own; he didn't know how and we hadn't yet provided him a way to—we sent him to school thinking everything was fine. Already, he was in a heightened state because his head hurt. On top of that, it was a show-and-tell day. We had been helping our son with his presentation so he'd be comfortable enough to give it. We picked a topic he liked, made sure he had some short and sweet sentences to use and made sure that the teacher understood not to push him or let the students badger him.

But when it came time for his presentation, he wanted nothing more than to be done with it—and the teacher didn't listen to us. She "encouraged" him to give the presentation. So with his anxiety, his discomfort, and his headache all at once, he ended up having an absolute fit right in the middle of the school day—and we went and picked him up because the school couldn't find a way to calm him down.

In this situation, the setting event was my son's headache. He was in a heightened state going in. The antecedent was that my son already didn't want to go and give this presentation. Those things combined, he needed to find a way to show that he needed to get out of there, but he was six and didn't have the language to do so, so he blew a fuse—the behavior. The consequence of that behavior was my wife and I going to pick him up.

Looking back at all I learned now, removing him from school that day was situationally the right thing, but long term, the wrong thing. Consequences are how children, autistic or not, learn what is effective as a behavior. Whether that behavior is positive or negative, if they get what they want, it reinforces that that behavior will be effective in providing the outcome that they're looking for. In this situation, we gave my son what he wanted—an out. It led to several more meltdowns that year until we were finally able to implement an IEP (individualized education plan) for him that helped to give him the time and space that he needed in school when he needed it and drastically increased his ability to remain at school.

Let me make note here that there are situations where those meltdowns are an indicator that the environment or situation isn't a positive one for your child. The key to these behavioral methods is knowing your child and knowing which ones are cries for help and which ones are being done because it worked the first time and neither their behavior or yours was corrected.

A key way to know when intervention and behavioral recalibrating is needed is by simply tracking when the meltdowns happen and the context for each one. Think of the journalistic questions: *who*, *what*, *where*, *when*, *why*, and sometimes *how*.

- Who was there when your child began to act out?
- What was happening before, during, or after they began to act out? (Was there a change in their routine? Did you indicate that something different was happening? Was a transition about to happen that they weren't prepared for?)
- Where did the meltdown happen? (Car, public, school, train, house—all of these will have different implications as to why your child might've become dysregulated.)
- When did this meltdown happen? (If it was earlier in the day, they might have needed more time to warm up to being awake. If it was toward the end, they might have been getting tired. Lunchtime, hungry. All of it is relevant.)
- Why do you think the meltdown happened? (Speculation can sometimes be good, but don't take this question too seriously. Additionally, if your child is able to communicate with you, ask them why they think it happened—after the fact, of course, and framed in a constructive way.)
- How did the meltdown happen? (This is a bit of a weird way to phrase it, but it simply means: Was it a screaming tantrum? A crying tantrum? Were they trying to injure themselves or someone else? Did they withdraw and shut down? All of these can help you to link patterns together to get to the root of what your child is trying to communicate through these situations.)

When all these questions as well as their answers are considered, it can be easier to determine when your child is acting out to communicate a need or acting out because they've been taught that that is an effective way to communicate. From there, you'll be able to determine where to begin behavior modification and start praising the behaviors you'd actually like to see be carried out in order to communicate wants or needs.

Punishment Versus Discipline

If you read my first book, *Raising Champions: A Roadmap to Success in ADHD Parenting*, then you'll remember the discussion over *punishment* and *discipline*. If you haven't read the first book, don't worry: I'm going to explain it again.

Put simply, the words *punishment* and *discipline* are often used synonymously to describe what's done when a child misbehaves, but the truth is that they each have a different implication attached to them, and one is actually better than the other—especially when it comes to parenting neurodivergent children. *Punishment* correlates specifically to what you think of when you think of the consequences dolled out to a child who's done wrong, such as grounding, being sent to their room, or taking away something that they enjoy. Generally speaking, the result is a very confused child, as they often don't understand how the punishment they've received relates to the wrongdoing they've committed—and they're often not taught the "proper" behavior to replace the "improper" one, so they're likely to do it again.

Discipline, on the other hand, refers to the kinder approach to changing behavior, when wrongdoing is explained, what was expected is explained, and perhaps a correlated and logical consequence is delivered. In these instances, the child knows exactly where things got off track and is given the tools necessary to correct themselves for next time so they know how to conduct themselves in the same situation going forward. The next section will focus mostly on discipline and how it can help to move your child in the right direction as opposed to punishment, which often has the opposite effect and can lead to the fracturing of parent-child relationships as well.

Promoting Positive Behavior

Promoting positive behaviors starts with understanding positive communication techniques and positive reinforcement. Punishment often doesn't make it very far with neurodivergent children because there's a lack of logical correlation between the action and the consequence, such as arguing with their sibling and then being sent to their room for it. In these cases, most times, the lesson won't be learned and the child will often be confused as to why they've been sent to their room to "think about what they did." They may consider instead that they understand why they did what they did and don't understand what they've done wrong—which is something that you need to consider as a parent and person trying to teach them. Instead, the goal of behavior modification is to substitute the less desirable behavior with a more positive one and explain that to your child. Give them a chance to correct it first before disciplining them—and when you do punish them, make the consequence correlate to the misbehavior so that it makes sense to them as to what they should have done instead.

Token Systems and Rewards

Token systems are a prime example of what positive reinforcement can look like. Usually, these token systems will be set up with a reward at the end, to be given out for the cost of a certain amount of tokens. These tokens are earned every time a particular task or behavior is carried out effectively. In this case, communicating with words rather than a scream could be a reason to get a token, or even pointing to their feelings on a visual chart rather than having an outburst. Whichever mode of communication is desired should be rewarded over what is not.

These tokens can take the form of any number of things, usually based on the age of your child. Younger children can usually benefit from a chart with stickers on it while older children may want to have something more tangible—maybe board game money they can later exchange for real money. The reward can also be decided between you and your child—again based on either your and their agreement and their age. Older children may want something specific at the grocery store, pick the movie on family movie night, or save up for an outing that's relevant to their special interests. Younger children may be content with getting an ice cream sandwich after five tokens or helping to craft the pizza on pizza night.

Redirecting Behavior

Another way to positively reinforce desirable over less desirable behavior is to redirect it. Let's say that your child is overwhelmed by the conversation that she's having with her father. She's trying to communicate how she's feeling, but her words are getting jumbled and her dad isn't understanding. In her frustration, she goes to hit herself in the leg—as many children with ASD tend to engage in self-injury in moments of frustration. To redirect the behavior, you take her hand and give her a nearby pillow. You understand that she's overwhelmed. She tried to communicate, but she wasn't able to do it, and she needed to let it out—but not on herself. The compromise is to give her the outlet—the pillow. It's not so much that you want to promote "violence," but you want to encourage a safer alternative to the frustration being let out than what was originally there. Over time, you could continue to substitute this for another, and then another behavior.

Visual Supports

It can also be helpful to provide your child with alternative ways to communicate their needs when words fail them. As it has hopefully been made clear by this point, communication is the main issue with many of those who struggle with ASD. They struggle with either their words, identifying their thoughts and feelings, or effectively conveying these things to other people in a way that's easily understood.

A happy medium that everyone understands is pictures. As the saying goes, "A picture is worth a thousand words." For those who struggle to communicate verbally, this truly is the case. Providing your child with alternative ways to communicate, such as a book of pictures that allows them to state their needs, their feelings, or their wants, can be the difference between a smiling child and a screaming one. Whether your child is verbal or nonverbal, these pictures can be very helpful when it comes to behavioral outbursts. Even mid-meltdown, if your child is struggling with communicating their needs and begins to spiral, you can bring the picture out and show them, ask them what they need, and potentially avoid the situation sliding any further into turmoil.

Providing Structure

Another key component to aiding children with ASD thrive is giving them the structure that their disorder demands of the world around them. Having the patience to provide your child with what they need can go a long way for them, especially when it comes to catering to their disorder. When it comes to this, though, it's definitely an easier-said-than-done deal, since there's so much about a day that can go haywire before you've even had a chance to have your morning coffee. Routine-oriented needs that autism often comes with mean that many a meltdown comes from a change in schedule, an unpredicted alteration to carefully constructed plans, or unforeseen circumstances that can throw the entire day into turmoil. Hence, this section will be broken down into two parts: First, having structure, and second, your backup plan.

Part One

Having set morning routines, set meal times, and set nighttime routines may sound like a lot, but it can be the difference between 2 and 12 meltdowns on a given day. ASD thrives on structure, so the more you have in a day, the better. It can be hard, of course, to predict what will go wrong and when—see Part Two below—but setting the day up with set waking times, set breakfast times, and set leaving-the-house times can help your child feel ready to tackle the day. Similarly, having a set night routine can make the transitions easier for your child so they know what's coming and what's expected of them at each point throughout the evening—when dinner is, how long after that they need to brush their teeth, when to get into their jammies, and when to get into bed for their night time story. This can also ensure they're getting as much sleep as possible at night to set them up for success the next day. For older children, this routine can be more independent but still integral to their daily success.

Part Two

Having as much structure in place as possible for your child while also being able to prepare them—and yourself—for the potential changes can go a long way for all of you. If you know that there are two potential outcomes to a particular day, communicate that as soon as possible with your child so they can prepare themselves for that possible change. If you know for a fact that something is going to throw a wrench in a routine for your child, communicate it as soon as possible and answer as many questions as you can for them. It can also be helpful every once in a while to change small parts of their routine so they can grow comfortable with some things not always happening exactly the way it was planned. Take this last step lightly, however, and consult with a professional—a therapist or your child's primary care physician—to see if this would be beneficial to your child, as not all children will find this beneficial to their disorder. The severity of some of their symptoms will determine this.

The Impact of "Poor Behavior"

Whether intentional or not, a child who misbehaves can cause stress and strain in any and all places where they interact with others. In many cases, those who interact with your child and understand their disorder will be compassionate and offer understanding and grace when they have meltdowns and moments where they lose their cool. Even those of us without a neurodevelopmental disorder lose our cool from time to time—it happens. In no way, shape, or form is it ever something I'd like to promote either where a child should be told not to express themselves or decompress when they need to—or worse, to change. However, when misbehavior becomes a mode of communication only rather than an extreme form of expression when they feel they have no other outlet, then there are secondary issues that can stem from this—and it's these extreme situations that are to be considered here.

Social

Children who act out often, such as by biting, hitting, or screaming at other children, often struggle to make or maintain friends. They can become lonely and in turn act out more, which can lead to a rather vicious cycle. This can lead to bullying, either from your child to others or onto your child from others. It can also lead to a poor self-image either way due to the isolation and lead, as well, to secondary conditions such as anxiety or depression. Helping your child to understand how to regulate their feelings when they don't feel seen or heard can help them to effectively communicate these needs with their friends without violence and lead to better understanding between peers and more successful relationships in the long run.

Academic (and Professional)

When children are taught that acting out gets them what they want—whether they were taught this intentionally or unintentionally—it can lead to children acting out in inappropriate places to get out of undesirable tasks, such as classrooms or even at work. It isn't so much that they're being intentional about this either; don't mistake this as an accusation that your child is manipulative. Take, for instance, the example of my son from earlier in the chapter. When we took him home from school, we taught him that tantrums would get him away from the discomfort that school causes him, and if he threw the tantrum, that bad feeling would go away. He associated the tantrums with relief from that negative experience, so he believed that if he continued to throw them, it would continue to bring that relief. He didn't believe that we were gullible and would do whatever we wanted because he cried, he just wanted the bad feeling to go away. The same thing can happen here. If your child learns to associate negative behaviors with positive consequences, they'll perform those behaviors to remove themselves from situations that cause them anxiety or distress. That's why it's important to give them the words or tools they need to communicate when they need to step away or need additional accommodations—such as an IEP to give them a private space to take tests or extra time to get the test done. This gives them control over the negative feeling without requiring a negative behavior to get the desired relief.

Familial

Similar to the two above, if a child associates negative behaviors with positive consequences, then they'll continue to execute that behavior. This can lead to tension within the household, tension among siblings, or anger toward your child because they don't "do what you want."

To Recap

It's important to remember two things: All children misbehave, and misbehavior in neurodivergent children often communicates a need. When it comes to your child's misbehavior, have grace and patience and try to get to the root of the issue first. Do your best not to give positive reinforcement to the negative behaviors, instead substituting those unwanted behaviors for more positive ones and then promoting those. You can do this through positive reinforcement techniques and praise. It can also be helpful to make sure that a routine is in place, both to help your child thrive, give them control over the things they're able to control, and to make sure that their basic needs—food, hygiene, and sleep—are being met to make sure that their baseline is as low as possible going into each day. The more people who are on board with these plans, the better as well. The next chapter will discuss IEPs and 504 plans to get the school involved and build that network for them, and Chapter 8 will focus on building your network as a parent to make sure everyone is being supported effectively.

Chapter 4:

Supporting Learning and Education

Learning disabilities are a common secondary condition to see pop up among neurodivergent children, though they aren't the only reason a child may struggle in school. Typically, learning disabilities compound already existing struggles—which means that even if your child isn't diagnosed with a learning disability, they may still be having difficulties.

Identifying Academic Struggles

Regardless of the cause of your child's academic difficulties, the first step to helping them with their studies is to know that they are having a hard time with them in the first place. This may be as simple as questioning them after a series of low grades, having meetings with their teachers, or monitoring their focus or frustration when it comes to completing their schoolwork at home. Projects and homework can be a good indicator of whether your child is grasping what they're learning in school or struggling with it. Younger children in particular may have a harder time hiding if they're struggling with their schoolwork so it can be easier to identify if there's an issue at hand.

Knowing When to Intervene

When it's clear that your child is having a hard time in school—be that from meetings with their teachers, discussions directly with your child about their experiences with school, or report cards that don't reflect the intelligence that you know your child has—it's time to step in. This hard time doesn't mean one low grade out of a bunch because they're having a hard time with a particular topic within a particular subject—it means pervasive difficulties with multiple areas either in multiple subjects or one particularly difficult one, depending on where their particular struggles may lie. Depending on where your child falls on the spectrum, they may have more or less difficulty with certain subjects or assignments as well. For instance, your child may do well with classwork because the teacher is right there to guide and instruct, but they may struggle with homework because of distractions, a lack of direction, or a lack of context, being away from where they learned the topic in the first place. They may also do fine with assignments and homework but have a hard time with tests because of the time restraints and demand for instant recall. Knowing how your child is affected by either their disorder or their learning disability can aid you in knowing when it's important to intervene as well as knowing *how* to do so to set your child up for the best chances of success.

Different Disabilities in Academia

There are a multitude of different disorders and disabilities that can affect your child in academic settings. The most common are dyslexia, dyscalculia, dysgraphia, and nonverbal learning disabilities that can affect concept correlation and understanding (Gehret, 2020).

Dyslexia

Dyslexia causes issues with comprehending written language. This means that reading is often a struggle, as those with dyslexia can experience the transposition of certain letters such as "b" and "d." As a result, children with dyslexia often read below grade level. Dyslexia can at times often cause additional communication issues as it overcomplicates word recognition and word sounds. None of this is to say that the child is less intelligent than their unaffected peers, but it does mean that learning to read will take more effort for them to be successful. This can lead to overwhelm when the task is presented and may lead to meltdowns as discussed in Chapter 3—specifically if the behavior warrants the removal of the negative stimuli (Mayo Clinic, 2022).

Dyscalculia

Dyscalculia is the inability to comprehend number-related information. Like those with dyslexia do with letters, those with dyscalculia will often experience the jumbling of numbers inside their head as they work to comprehend what's written in front of them. This means that what may seem like simple math to one child may seem like a torture device for another (Cleveland Clinic, 2022-b).

Dysgraphia

Though it's not as common for children with ASD to have issues with their general motor function, their fine motor function can often be affected by their disorder. This can result in something known as dysgraphia. Dysgraphia truly is a two-part disorder as it has both a motor and a thought component. The motor component deals with the child's ability to actually write words or figures out on a piece of paper. With dysgraphia, their ability to form these shapes may be compromised, meaning that what they write may appear in poor penmanship or even be entirely illegible. Compounding this is the second part of this disorder, which poses challenges to a child's ability to translate their internal thoughts into an external medium. This means that when a child thinks of the sentence "I'd like a sandwich," they may struggle to put those words into figures and a pen to paper to actually write that sentence down. This can lead to out-of-order letters or words and poorly structured sentences. It may also be hard to read what they've written. Dysgraphia can cause many issues, such as difficulty with completing assignments or writing notes down (Cleveland Clinic, 2022-a). They may also struggle with written communication—meaning that if they're nonverbal and struggle to write, there's one less way for them to communicate their needs effectively.

Nonverbal Learning Disability

Nonverbal learning disability (NLD or NVDL) is not currently recognized by the *Diagnostic and Statistical Manual of Mental Disorders (DSM-V)*, but research has shown that it affects as many as three million children (Margolis et. al., 2020). Often, children who have NLD are diagnosed—either mistakenly or instead of, meaning they have both—with ADHD or ASD as the symptoms are shared among the three disorders.

With NLD, children will struggle with things like spatial awareness or visual learning, meaning they may have a hard time with depth perception or with translating drawn images as they are simply unable to perceive them (Miller, 2023). Those with NLD may also struggle with what is known as "high-order comprehension," which simply means the ability to process what the most important information is in a lecture, book, or set of data presented to them (Miller, 2023). This means that when children are trying to take notes in class, they may not know what they're supposed to be writing down, so their notes may become overwhelming with "irrelevant" information, or they may not have enough information to go off of in order to complete their homework or study. Moreover, when working on certain assignments, they may not understand how certain concepts connect together, such as how different plot points lead to a conflict or a resolution in a story, which can lead to difficulty in reading and comprehension classes (Miller, 2023). This struggle with comprehension can also bleed over to math skills, where identifying patterns and concept connections is important.

Where the confusion ties into both ASD and ADHD, though, is how NLD can affect a child's social communication and executive functioning skills. Executive functioning is all of those skills that allow us to prioritize, plan, and motivate ourselves to get things done. In neurotypical people, many executive functions happen without us thinking about them. As discussed in book one, *Raising Champions: A Roadmap to Success in ADHD Parenting,* those with ADHD struggle with their executive functioning in almost every major way because of the way the disorder affects their brain development and function. With NLD, it's very similar. Those who struggle with NLD in turn struggle with the ability to break things down into smaller tasks in order to prioritize what needs to be done first and foremost in order to complete those larger responsibilities (Miller, 2023). In most cases, this means that this task will never get done.

Those with NLD may also struggle with the ability to read facial expressions or body language, meaning that when it comes to social settings, they're often left in the dark (Miller, 2023). As explained in Chapter 1 and in Chapter 2 of this book, communication issues are the prime symptom of autism. Hence, NLD often hides in plain sight—especially in children who have already been diagnosed with autism.

A key to identifying if your child is struggling with NLD in addition to their autism is watching for when the symptoms set in. In many cases, the social issues may be persistent, as this is what motivates most parents or professionals to have their child tested in their earlier years for autism, so it isn't a proper indicator of autism. Neither are math struggles on their own. But if these issues suddenly crop up when your child reaches their middle school years—around fifth or sixth grade—this is a good indicator that a secondary issue, namely NLD, is present (Miller, 2023). The reason for this is that, in earlier years, many children with NLD were able to get by due to memorization alone. Early education focuses on basic math and learning to read. They're able to learn how to read the words on the page and to memorize how to do the work on the page in their math classes—though they may not exactly understand why. Later, though, reading classes change from learning to reading to learning how to comprehend what they're reading—and that's when the struggle begins. It's the same thing with math classes. So, if your child suddenly starts to struggle in these middle school years, it can be a good indication that additional testing should be done.

Honorable Mention: Savant Syndrome

Savant syndrome was mentioned once before in Chapter 1 when discussing co-occurring disorders—and while it's not technically a learning disability, it was worth mentioning here because of the implications that it can have on your child's ability to learn. Oftentimes, those with savant syndrome are particularly skilled in one subject—let's say math in this instance. Your child may thrive in math to the point where they're like a walking calculator. An example of this would be Sheldon from *Young Sheldon.* Another example is Patrick Obeyedkov from an episode of *House* who was a savant at playing the piano. Savants are particularly skilled in one (or sometimes many) areas—but they often struggle in others. In many cases with savant syndrome, much of the child's talent lies with their special skill and deprives them in other areas. So, while your child may thrive in math, they may have dyslexia and thus struggle to read. Alternatively, your child could thrive in their art classes but have zero ability to grasp the concept of algebra.

It's important to remember that savant syndrome affects about only 1 out of every 10 children with ASD—but that's still quite a high number considering how frequently it affects the general populace, so it's worth keeping an eye on.

Promoting Your Child's Academic Success

If it becomes apparent that your child has something else going on that's complicating their school experience, then the best thing to do for them is to get them the help that they need in order to succeed. In many cases, this means enrolling them with tutors, therapists, and other professionals who can help them in the areas that they may be struggling. It also means that an IEP is necessary.

Collaborating With Professionals

Professionals like tutors, therapists, and classroom aids can be beneficial to your child's academic studies because they can offer personalized support for your child's specific needs. Tutors, unlike teachers, are able to customize their "lesson plan" to the type of help that your child needs. For instance, if your child struggles immensely with algebra but is a whiz at trigonometry, then they can focus on the FOIL method rather than the Pythagorean theorem—whereas in a classroom (or at least when *I* went to school), the Pythagorean theorem was the arch nemeses for most of us, but we could FOIL until the sun went down. The FOIL method is a mnemonic device used to help remember how to multiply binomials in math—first, outside, inside, last. Take the following equation for example:

$$(a + b)(c + d) = ?$$

To get the answer, you would need to FOIL the two binomials together. To FOIL it would mean to take the first from each binomial—*a* and *c*—and multiply them together, then take the outside terms—*a* and *d*—then the inside—*b* and *c*—and finally the last—*b* and *d*. The result would be your answer:

$$ac + ad + bc + bd$$

In that setting, my son would have been in a bad way in either case since he hated math no matter what it was.

Therapists can also be helpful in this case because if your child's academic struggles come from being overwhelmed in the classroom more than the actual academic struggles, they can offer your child coping mechanisms or alternative methods to gaining the information that they need. They can also give your child a space to decompress—referring here to a school counselor or safe space in the school building. My son's high school had general guidance counselors but also paid a licensed therapist to come in once a week to offer support to the children, and he always got a slot in the afternoon to go and unwind after a long week—it was built into his IEP.

Classroom aids can also be a great help to younger children because they can help to maintain focus, help with being trained in how your child communicates so they can help meet your child's needs when the teacher is assisting the others in the room, and help to provide school to home communication. In many cases, the aid is there primarily to support your child, then secondarily to support the teacher and the parent in facilitating effective communication between all parties involved.

Individualized Education Plans (IEPs)

Many of the professionals mentioned above can be mandated by way of an IEP, which we've touched on a few times now. The Individuals With Disabilities Act (IDEA) is what gives access to these accommodations (Bailey, 2021). IEPs can be given out to any child who falls under 1 of the 13 qualifying categories—one of which is autism spectrum disorder (Bailey, 2021). With IEPs, any and all accommodations that your child may need in order to succeed in school can be detailed out. These requests can be as simple as extra time on tests or as complex as time periods to leave the room, extra space around their desks in order to have room to move or stim if they need it, or even mandated notes home every day to report on how your child's day went and if there were any problems or pain points.

IEPs are generally negotiated between the parents, the school's special education coordinator, a guidance counselor who is familiar with your child and their needs or a therapist who can serve the same purpose, and a child if they're old enough or cognizant enough to contribute (Bailey, 2021). This is a legally binding document that's reviewed, revised, and updated each year, and if it's revealed that the IEP accommodations aren't being met, you do have the right to request an investigation and pursue legal action if the reasons as to why it's not being followed aren't merited (Bailey, 2021).

One of the other major benefits that are offered by IEPs that will come back up later in the book is that many IEPs, especially for older children like teens in high school, offer help with accommodating to life even beyond school, so the transition from academia to adulthood is smoother and easier to cope with.

Positive Learning Settings at Home

Another major factor to academic success when it comes to your child is making sure that their needs are being met even when they aren't in school. This means making sure they have a quiet space to work at home, all the materials that they need to complete their work at home, and the structure and support that they need to complete those tasks as well. For some children, this may mean doing work with you in the same room and with your help to do it either verbally or on paper. For others, it may mean having periodic check-ins, or even just having you review it at the end. In certain circumstances, doing it at home may not be constructive at all, and working at the library may be more conducive to their needs. Your child will be able to show you what they need, which is why it is important to always check in with them and see what would best suit their needs.

To Recap

Children with autism may struggle with their academics for a plethora of reasons, either pertaining to their ASD or because of the many co-occurring learning disabilities that they may also have. Early diagnosis and intervention are important, but constant communication with the professionals in your child's life and your child is just as key to making sure that your child's needs are being met and they're still succeeding in the best way that they're able. In-school support, a network of professionals, and at-home support, are all key to making this happen.

Chapter 5:

Nurturing Emotional Well-Being

Autism is a difficult disorder to live with. There's no way to sugarcoat that. There will be days when every sound is sandpaper in your child's ears, where no piece of clothing will sit correctly on their skin when they won't be able to find a single thing to eat that will suit their needs. There will be meltdowns, mute days, and bad days all around. While the good days need to be acknowledged and cherished and held in high regard because they're what we always strive for, it's the bad days that we need to prepare for and prepare our children for, so that they don't step into the pitfalls that may come with their disorder in the long term.

That's where building your child's self-esteem comes in. Self-esteem is what helps your child to be sure of themselves and their decisions and to not collapse onto themselves when things go wrong. This isn't to say that being confident will make their skin stop itching when those clothes fail to cooperate, but it will help them to know they're allowed to step away and change if they need to, to go sit down and unwind if it becomes too much, and to understand that because they need to accommodate themselves, they shouldn't feel othered or ostracized because of it. Building their self-assuredness, self-awareness, and self-confidence will help them to cope better when things go wrong and to handle the challenges that come with their disorder in the long term.

Autism and Self-Esteem

How your child's autism affects their self-esteem will be dependent entirely on their symptoms as well as their ability to cope with them. For children who are more aware of their deficits and are in turn more aware of when they're being othered, they may struggle more to maintain a positive attitude when things take a turn with their friends or in larger social settings. For children who are less aware of the external pressures, they may still have a hard time with understanding their symptoms, with understanding why it had to be them to have this disorder, or why they have to struggle with the symptoms that they do, but they may more easily release the societal pressure that comes with all of that. No matter where your child falls on the spectrum, they will most likely struggle with their self-worth and self-image at some point. This is why it's important to always promote positivity to your child when it comes to their disorder. Even when being positive is the farthest thing from your mind (and it does happen—being the parent of a neurodivergent child is difficult, which will be discussed in the last chapter), it's important to maintain that positivity for them. Disorders like autism can rob your child of their autonomy and control, which can also make them feel like less. This can in turn make a negative self-image come to light and make, as well, for a plethora of secondary conditions like depression or anxiety.

What Low Self-Esteem Looks Like

Understanding what low self-esteem looks like is integral to knowing when it may be important to step in and help your child. Remember that symptoms may appear differently for every child—and the symptoms that your child experiences with their autism may affect how these symptoms present as well, so always consult with professionals. The following is meant to give you a chance to understand when it may be time to get those professionals involved.

Self-esteem isn't something that will disappear overnight. You may not even realize the change right away, but instead, look back one day and realize that your kid, who was once rambunctious and energetic, is suddenly sullen and reserved. This is a major red flag.

Generally speaking, when a child is suffering from low self-esteem, it stems from them accepting the comments made about them by other people—usually negative—or coming to a conclusion that they don't fit in with those around them. With autism, either is possible or even both. They may not even realize themselves that they've taken on the negative views of others. Instead, it may simply be a snide comment here or there that's mostly meant as a joke, yet has just a little bit of truth behind it.

This negativity may devolve slowly until they begin to believe it, truly seeing themselves as lesser. This would appear as them making their needs smaller in favor of others, becoming introverted or reserved, or even becoming shy or meek where they may not have been before. Things like people-pleasing are common in children with low self-esteem, to the point where they may compromise their morals or values in order to make sure that they stay in favor of their peers. In other cases, they may even lash out angrily when someone tries to give them praise or positive feedback, as they don't feel they deserve it or that it's the truth.

In extreme cases, depression can become an issue. If your child's sleep patterns, appetite, or mood become drastically altered in addition to the above, professional intervention may be necessary to make sure that your child gets the help they need.

Building Positive Self-Esteem

The first step to helping your child build their self-esteem is to make sure that you have a positive relationship with them—a relationship that they're comfortable sharing with you. Parents often believe that no matter the status of their relationship, their children will share with them if something goes horribly amiss. This way of thinking, though, is a prime example of how things can slip through the cracks. Even in cases where you have a wholly positive relationship with your child, they may feel that because their experience is something they will always need to live with, it's not worth complaining about and they may keep things to themselves. So, before all else, it's important to make sure your child knows that they can come to you, even with the most seemingly futile of things, that they will be heard and listened to, and that you'll be there to validate them and offer solutions should they want them.

Building their confidence in their abilities comes from other places as well, though—namely with receiving the support that they need while interacting with the world around them.

Praise

One of the key ways that you can help your child maintain their self-esteem is by praising them when they do something well (Wakeling, 2020). Praising children for every little thing can sometimes seem like overkill, to the point where it might seem condescending, but for children who struggle with the same usual interactions that neurotypical children might, these smaller wins are worthy of this abundance of praise. It can show them that while they may struggle in some areas, there are still other areas where they succeed and maybe even excel. More than that, it can help to give your child the opportunity to engage in activities that they enjoy and that they know they're good at so that they don't feel challenged all the time or that they're constantly at a deficit (Wakeling, 2020). Children always need the chance to feel accomplished—but especially children who struggle with those tasks that may be seen as "normal" to most of the world.

Positive Reinforcement

This praise should also be given every time a child does what they're asked, reacts to something in a positive way, or even removes themselves from a situation where they might have otherwise acted negatively. This aligns with the behavioral chapter where tokens and rewards were discussed, but it takes it a step further by adding verbal confirmation from the parents in those gaps where tokens or rewards might not be necessary. In those moments where an award isn't given but the behavior is still positive, praise should still be given as all wins should be acknowledged. In this context, it may be referred to as positive reinforcement, but the concept of how that is delivered is the same as above. This helps promote those positive behaviors and also helps to promote your child's confidence in themselves and the decisions that they make in those moments. Their strengths should always be supported and encouraged, and opportunities should always be given for them to be able to show off these talents and skills at any point.

Parental Reflective Functioning

Another way that might help you as a parent to be there for your child is something called parental reflective functioning, or PRF. This is actually an ADHD parenting technique, but it can be equally helpful with ASD, as I learned with my son, because it is designed to help you pay attention to your child's cues as to when they might be experiencing distress (Children and Adults With Attention-Deficit/Hyperactivity Disorder [CHADD], 2018). PRF encourages you as the parent to learn their tells of when a meltdown is coming so you can step in before they fall off the deep end and hopefully introduce a coping mechanism or redirect the behavior (CHADD, 2018).

At the end of the day, showing your child that you're there for them, that you're supporting them, and that you love them no matter what will help them through the hardest of it. Understanding that they have someone in their corner will always help them when it comes to the challenges they face because they won't feel like they're going through it alone. Having other families with children who are sharing the experience may also be beneficial to your child as they get older so they know that they aren't the only one in the world going through what they're going through.

Allowing Certain Behaviors

Children with autism interact with the world in a very particular way—specifically in the way that they process information and regulate themselves as they take it in. This may be by monologuing about their special interests, stimming—or participating in repetitive behaviors—when they get excited, or even repeating certain phrases, facts, or questions as a way of communicating. One of the most positive ways that you can help your child be comfortable in their skin is by not trying to alter these behaviors.

In their day-to-day lives in the world, your child will be forced into a mold so that they appear "normal" like the rest of us—usually referred to as masking. This may mean that they can't stim, won't monologue, and may hold conversations that make them uncomfortable just to fit in. It may make them feel fake, put them off, or set them up for meltdowns later in the day.

By allowing them the space to tell you about the things they enjoy in a format they're comfortable with, such as monologuing, you're telling them that you're a safe person to speak to and that it's okay for them to communicate in such a way. More than that, if your child is stimming while they talk, don't tell them to stop. In many cases, these stims are not harmful and are usually contained to the space your child occupies—so let them do it. Telling them not to can make them feel othered the same way they might in other places in the world and it may lead to distrust between you and them. It can also be beneficial to you to learn how they communicate, so you know if their repeating of a question is actually them answering it, if their echoing of a sentence is something relevant or just because they liked the way the words sounded, or if their stating of a fact they read off the internet is a prompt for a longer conversation or just an interesting fact. Don't force them to be more than what they are, and don't ask them to be less than what they are when in a safe space.

Seeking Professional Help

As mentioned in the symptoms section of this chapter, professional opinions and even intervention are sometimes needed to make sure that your child is getting the appropriate treatment for their symptoms if it turns out that there is something more going on. In cases of low self-esteem, anxiety, and depression separate from their autism can become an issue that compounds the entire experience. Therapy can be a helpful space for your child to feel heard and to gain additional coping skills for the additional challenges that anxiety and depression may pose for them.

For children who have anxiety and depression before their self-esteem is affected, having professional opinions and intervention already in place can be a helpful way to keep your child's confidence up and their lines of communication open so that, should something go awry, there's already someone at the ready to lend them an ear and some aid.

Something to Keep in Mind

I mentioned this in the self-esteem chapter in my first book, but I need to reiterate it here because it is so important. When it comes to neurodivergent children, they will run into people who expect them to be "less" every single day. When they're experiencing the world cranked to a 10, they're also living at a 10, and everyone expects them to turn themselves back down to a 5.

Don't be one of these people.

A child who misbehaves is always going to cause frustration. That frustration can be compounded by fear that if you're not able to teach your child how they're supposed to behave, they'll struggle with these problems persistently and it will lead to conflict in their academic and professional lives as well. The thing to remember in both of these scenarios is that your child is living with a complicated disorder, which can cause difficulties and problems with behavior. It isn't so simple as being a "good" or "bad" kid; there are far more complex things at play. Autism makes things difficult to handle, and while it can be managed and can be lived with without being fixed, it can also sometimes be in charge rather than your child, and you have to give them the space to let that happen.

Remember that they don't always need to be disciplined, sometimes just reminded. Remember that they don't always mean to say something rude, they just didn't know that it was rude to say. And remember that sometimes the chicken just tastes too much like chicken—and there's nothing that can be done about it.

The things to remind yourself are that even parents of neurotypical children struggle with their children's behavior, with what they say, and with what they eat. With neurodivergent children, the difference is that they don't always understand that these aren't acceptable behaviors, and they will take the reprimand to heart. So, as much as you can, let some things go. One of the sentiments that we use a lot in my household, despite its overuse, is "Pick your battles." Be sure to also read Chapter 8 to see how important it is to network as a parent of a child with autism so that you don't experience the burnout and stress that can come with being the parent of a neurodivergent child as well.

To Recap

Autism can affect your child's self-esteem in a number of ways—from making them feel ostracized in social settings to making them feel out of control of their own bodies without understanding the reason. The most important thing that you can do is celebrate their wins, no matter how small, and encourage them through their losses. Remember to always have a door open for them so they know that you are a safe space. Don't speak out in front of them about the challenges you face with their disorder—there are other times and other places for that. Don't make them feel lesser for being who they are. Always allow them the space and grace to be whoever they are. Letting them know that who they are is perfectly okay is the first step in making sure your child is confident in who they are.

Chapter 6:

Promoting Independence and Life Skills

By promoting a child's self-esteem when it comes to their disorder, you're also setting your child up for being able to succeed in their adult life, at a time when they're more reliant on themselves and their own capabilities and less on other people. It's a myth that people with autism can't lead successful and independent lives. Though it is true that some with the disorder will need consistent intervention and aid throughout their lives, it is not true that their lives will be any less fulfilling than their neurotypical peers. This fulfillment, however, is dependent on your child's ability to complete tasks on their own and know that they can rely on themselves for assurance when the going gets tough. Having confidence in themselves is the first step to becoming independent. The rest from that point is much easier to handle.

Preparing Your Child With ASD for Independence

Many of the tips and tricks in this book can be outfitted to help your child begin to do things for themselves, though that may not have been the original intention for them to be included. For instance, Chapter 3 was included to help promote positive coping skills and behavioral patterns, but it can also be used in some ways to help teach your child particular skills that will help them later on in life. Similarly, helping your child to get a grasp on social conventions and communication will help them when it comes to getting and maintaining a job, finding roommates if that's something they might need, or even dealing with normal communication like shopping at the grocery store. All of these small tools can be useful for promoting independence, the same as with a neurotypical child, just with a couple of extra motivators and steps.

Chores and Independence

No one likes to do chores. More than that, no one likes to do chores that they don't understand. This is why chores can be an important part of your household because they can both show you what your child still needs to learn and also give your child the space to interact with the things that are needed to keep a household running. Teaching them how to sweep, mop, wash dishes, do their laundry, and clean different parts of the house like sinks, toilets, bathtubs, and appliances can help your child to get a grasp on all the different ways that a house needs to be taken care of. It can also give them the different skills they might need to apply them to other aspects of their lives, such as jobs. Bathrooms are cleaned the same pretty universally, as are floors and countertops, so if you teach your child to do this at home, they're able to do it anywhere. However, if they never learn how to do these things—how often to do them, what products to use, and what tools are needed to get those surfaces clean—then they may be less likely to do them, know that they need to be done, or even understand that that's a task that should be kept on their radar. The goal will ultimately be to teach them the skills they need for daily living.

Stepping away from my son for a second, I'll provide an example from my own childhood. It's a simple thing, but as a child, I was never taught how to properly clean a carpet. My childhood home only had hardwood floors, so I'd never had any reason to learn the skill—it was simply a matter of circumstance. Unfortunately, in my first apartment when I moved out, I had carpeting in the bedroom, and within my first week of living there, I spilled a soda on it (eating in the bedroom was something I had been reprimanded for as a child; it was a lesson I *chose* not to learn, but that's a different story). Suddenly, I was in need of that knowledge, but I didn't have it, and I needed to call my mother to teach me how to do it—and she laughed at me because I didn't know how. Instead of offering to help, she told me I needed to learn and hung up. I ended up cleaning it incorrectly based on a few articles online and bleaching the carpet, so it was permanently stained. I didn't clean the carpet again the entire time I lived there, and not again until I met my wife and she taught me how to properly do it.

The point of including this story is to exemplify two things: The first is that if your child isn't taught how to do something, then they won't know how to do it—especially if they're never confronted with that need. Like with me and that carpet, I had never needed to learn, so I never did. Second, it will never be conducive to laughing at your child for not knowing something. Even I, a neurotypical person, struggled with that reaction from my mother because there had never been a reason for me to know that information, and she was aware of that fact, so it was unnecessary ridicule. For neurodivergent children, who often struggle with tasks that may be considered relatively commonplace and mundane, laughing will show them that they're othered, wrong, or may make them feel less intelligent and unsupported.

It's important to always give children the opportunity to ask questions and to learn, even when the question may seem silly or the task commonplace, because they may have never needed to learn that skill up to that point. Moreover, the more that they're asked to do, no matter how "unfun" it may seem, the better prepared they'll be to care for their own space in the long run.

Mock Conversations

This idea was left out of Chapter 2 because it wasn't the most conducive to helping your child learn how to communicate—at least, it wasn't with my son, who often felt that these mock conversations put more pressure on him and left him struggling when it came to learning how to communicate.

When it came to preparing for real-world situations later in life, however, like job interviews, practicing for his road test, and interacting with his first girlfriend's parents, these mock conversations were a huge help to him because they helped him to understand more of how the script would go. As mentioned in Chapter 2, having scripts at the ready is a huge help for children with autism, and in these highly formulated settings, these scripts were very helpful for my son. We would practice interviews, practice him meeting his friend's parents, and even practice interactions with his teachers if he was particularly nervous about starting a new class from year to year. These things made the transitions easier for him and gave him something to fall back on if he suddenly found himself struggling with the situation at hand.

While it may seem silly to rehearse real-life situations that could go any one of a million ways, these different scenarios can help your child to prepare for these different outcomes and even understand how to read if a conversation is going positively or negatively, or if something is rhetorical or a prompt for them to start talking. Even if the conversation doesn't go exactly as rehearsed, they'll have something of a cheat sheet to refer back to in terms of body language and tone, so they won't be so in the dark about what's happening around them.

Errands

For many children with autism, overstimulation or dysregulation comes from the unpredictability of everyday life. This may seem like an oxymoron because if the same things happen every day, then it can't be unpredictable. The thing is that there are always slight variations to our routines—heavier traffic than usual, needing to stop at the grocery store before coming right home, a doctor's appointment that you forgot about, your child needing to get picked up because they're sick—it's inevitable.

Another way that you can prepare your child for independence is by helping them to embrace these unplanned changes. For younger children, this may be as simple as not always telling them when a change is going to happen and then talking them through regulation techniques.

This isn't always recommended for younger children, though, as autism isn't something that will get better through exposure therapy. But for older children who are already doing things on their own—maybe driving themselves to school or just spending more time away from the house—it can be good to try to offer them different ways to get into places where they may experience some discomfort. Send them to the grocery store to do the shopping for you. Send them to the doctor's on their own for the first time. Ask them to stop on their way home from school for something. These small hiccups can be helpful in preparing them for all the different things they'll need to take care of on their own when they're no longer in the house.

Money Management

The other benefit of errands is to help your child learn money management. Sending them to the store with a budget will help them understand the importance of knowing what to buy, understanding the value of money, and understanding how to buy one product for multiple meals to help maximize the cost of certain products.

Another way to encourage this is to have them help you balance your checkbook. Even though no one really keeps up with this anymore, it can be another way for your child to visualize the inflow and outflow of money in your bank account and understand where that money goes. They may also be part of the bill-paying process so they can understand how that needs to be accomplished, be it online or via writing a check. It can help to conceptualize how keeping the house running works financially as well as physically.

How IEPs Can Help

As we've discussed previously, IEPs can be exceptionally helpful, and in this case, they can help set your child up for success in adulthood. Though they will end when your child graduates high school, they can help to start your child on the path toward successful adult independence. Many parents will put this plan into effect in middle school, though it can be started at any point before your child turns 16 (McKinney, 2021). The IEP planners will take your child's goals into account and set the course that will best set them up to be able to achieve those goals. It's also important to allow your child to have an active role in their IEP planning and meetings so that they understand what is going on with their education as well as their transition planning. The other thing to keep in mind is that, in all likelihood, your child will end up in charge of their IEP before they graduate high school. So long as they are of sound mind and under the age of 22, IEP decisions will fall to that of your child as soon as they turn 18, right up until they graduate high school (Lee, 2020). If they don't have an understanding of what's going on with their education or with them, there's no guarantee that the transition will go smoothly, so the more involved they are, the better things will be in the long term.

Transition plans drawn up in IEPs can help your child in any of their goals, including college, trade school, or finding a job, be that job on their own accord or through another disabilities support system (Center for Parent Information and Resources, n.d.). If your child will need additional adult support, a Chapter 688 can be filed to help them get aid as an adult (Massachusetts Department of Elementary and Secondary Education, 2015).

Disclaimer

I'd like to add a disclaimer about this section though. It can be incredibly important to have your child do things on their own—but always be mindful of their limits. Children with autism are still autistic, so there may be days when it's simply too much to ask this of them. These tasks may also be dependent on their symptoms and if this is something they're physically or mentally capable of completing on their own. Always be sure to consider your child and if this is within their means. If you're not sure, consult with your child about if it's something they'd be comfortable with—or if they're not yet old enough to comment on the situation, consult with professionals who are involved with their lives to see if it's something that they recommend.

It's important to note again that autism is a spectrum, hence why it is called autism *spectrum* disorder. This means that while some children may be able to grow up to live on their own, have successful careers, and form long-lasting friendships and relationships, others may only succeed in one of these areas or perhaps none of them. This doesn't mean that those who remain dependent on caregivers are living less fulfilling lives—it just means that they need more help in their day-to-day activities to achieve that fulfillment. Considering where your child falls on that spectrum is important when it comes to deciding what type of aid to offer them as they develop to different levels of maturity and eventually transition to taking care of themselves, if that's a step they'll be able to take.

How Routines Help With Independence

Routines are a big part of life for those with autism. They're a way to help regulate behavior, avoid meltdowns, and keep things comfortable for those who struggle with the disorder. Routines have another advantage, however, and that's helping to ease the transition into adulthood for older teens who are working their way up to being in charge of themselves.

It may seem counterproductive, as you try to force your child into the structure while also trying to prepare them for the lack of structure that is the real world, but giving your child something to hold onto can actually make the transition easier because it can give them something consistent to return back to as everything else is thrown into flux. They may understand that they'll always eat dinner at 6 p.m. even if things are completely in turmoil. No matter what the day brings them, they can shower before bed to help them calm down. They'll always know that the next day, they'll have toast for breakfast, so they'll be fed and comfortable even if work is determined to be utter chaos the next day. Routines help things remain certain even in a mass of uncertainty.

More than that, though, routines can help your child understand the things that need to be accomplished throughout the day without forgetting what needs to be done, so even if they're not 100% independent, they can still maintain a little sense of them being able to do certain things on their own. If your child understands that when they wake up in the morning, the first three things they need to do are use the bathroom, brush their teeth, and take their medicine—and their brain thrives on structure—then it can be assumed that every morning, they'll get up, use the bathroom, brush their teeth, and take their medicine without incident. Unlike children with ADHD who often need to be reminded of the things that need to be done in a given day, children with autism will stick to the routines that they're given because rules and regiments are what give them comfort and understanding in a world that tends not to make much sense to them.

To Recap

Transitioning into being independent is difficult for any child, but it can be particularly challenging for children with autism because of the way that the world counteracts with the way their disorder manifests. There is no routine to the world and there is no one easy way to communicate or interact with each scenario that makes it easy for those who struggle. By giving children the tools to be as independent as possible, though, you can prepare them for as much as you can in terms of what to expect in their adult lives. Chores, errands, and practice conversations can help give your child a leg-up in day-to-day scenarios they'll run into, so they'll never be quite without a blueprint for what to expect when it comes to adulthood. Moreover, they'll be prepared via the routines that have dominated much of their childhood, so they'll understand what they need to do even if things don't go exactly as planned.

Chapter 7:

Thriving as a Family

Something to keep in mind when it comes to one of your children receiving an autism diagnosis is that the entire family will feel the effects. As a parent, it's a given that you understand this. Being that you are your child's main advocate and you have taken up the mantle of understanding their disorder and bearing that burden with them, you understand more than anyone else what it's like to live with someone who has autism. But the thing to remember is that it isn't just you who experiences these stresses. First and foremost, your diagnosed child is experiencing everything on the front lines. They deal with their symptoms, the challenges those symptoms bring, and the consequences of their disorder on a daily basis. Then comes the second line of defense: you. You and your partner deal with professional aid such as IEPs, therapists, and doctor's appointments. You also offer the emotional support your child may need at any given point and stand between them and the really bad days so that they can better be prepared to cope with them.

There is still another line of defense, though, that whether intended or not, ends up taking the brunt of your child's autism. That's the other people living in your house, be it your other children or grandparents who may live with you. (For the sake of simplicity, the focus will be on other siblings in the household, but bear in mind the other people as well, so you can know when to offer them support and aid too.) Though they do not have autism themselves and are not involved in the primary caregiving of your autistic child, they are on the receiving end of their symptoms, of the challenges that come with those symptoms, and of the consequences of any bad days or meltdowns that may crop up from their disorder. This adds tension and stress between them and their autistic sibling and also you and them because of perceptions of expectation and favoritism. A lot of this can be avoided with communication, of course, but the important thing is how exactly to communicate about such an important thing, and how to do it effectively so hurt feelings are avoided and no one is asked to compromise themselves for the benefit of another without something in return.

Explaining Autism to Your Other Children

As with most topics discussed in this book, the first step to open and effective communication is making sure that everyone understands exactly what's being talked about—in this case, making sure that everyone understands what autism is and what challenges an autism diagnosis poses. The trick here is to make the subject approachable to your child, meaning you may need to explain it in a simpler way for your children who are younger.

This may mean that for your younger children, autism could be described as follows:

"Sometimes your sibling has trouble communicating how they're feeling. This means that sometimes they may yell or throw things even when we know it isn't okay. They may also not always know what to say, and they may get upset when things aren't the way that they like them."

For older children, you can add more details, become more technical, and get more specific with your explanation to better explain the exact situation that your family may experience due to your specific child's symptoms and experience.

Regardless of how you need to explain it, by the end, the end goal is to make sure that they understand three things:

1. what autism is
2. how it affects their diagnosed sibling
3. how it affects them

With these three goals checked off, they'll be better prepared for the challenges that the diagnosis poses and be more prepared for the "role" that they play in your family dynamic.

I want to clarify here that by "role" I am stating more generally the part they play in accommodating their diagnosed sibling's needs when that becomes necessary, not that they're expected to behave or act a specific way just because they live in the same household as a child with a disability. Just as hard as we try to make sure our neurotypical children aren't othered, so too should we maintain that same attitude with our neurotypical children. The goal is not favoritism toward one or the other but an agreement among all parties so that there's stasis within the family unity. The use of the term *role* is simply meant as a placeholder, since there isn't a better, more concise word to use for what it is I'm trying to explain.

Involving Your Other Children in the Diagnosis

The final part of the above that wasn't explained there deliberately involves your neurotypical children in your neurodivergent child's diagnosis. This literally means letting them help where they can and interact with their sibling as normally as they're able and bringing them into the fold as normally as one might if they were to have a neurotypical sibling. Allow them to understand that their sibling may face challenges, but let them also act like siblings with them. Being autistic doesn't prevent your child from still being a child, after all.

The other component of "involving your children in the diagnosis" is making sure they understand how to live with someone who's been diagnosed with autism. By explaining to them what living with someone who has autism means, they'll be able to better prepare themselves for the different scenarios they may find themselves in and may be able to better prepare for when they need to call upon those skills.

What Challenges and Frustrations They May Face

Your other children may face certain situations that differ from yours as a sibling of someone with autism rather than being a parent of someone with autism. Similar to being a parent of a neurotypical child and a sibling of a neurotypical child, your relationship with your child with autism differs, so the way that you interact with them will differ as well. Your expectations as a parent primarily are advocacy and care, but siblings expect that they'll have a playmate, someone to commiserate with when they feel you're being unjust (even if you aren't or don't think you are), and someone to laugh or cry with when something difficult happens in their lives. Siblings provide a constant for your children—someone who's always there for them and at their level to provide comfort and love with. When one of those siblings has autism, however, some of those expected interactions are interrupted by the challenges that autism presents.

For starters, not every child with autism is able to participate in play the way a neurotypical child may expect, want, or even need. Your child with autism may not be able to comprehend the game that your other child would like to play because they simply can't comprehend the imaginary component. Similarly, they may not understand the rules if they're too ambiguous. This can lead to conflict or confusion, a fight between the siblings, or a meltdown on your autistic child's part. For those children who are more aware of their symptoms, it may lead to guilt on either side—from the neurotypical sibling for pushing too hard and from the neurodivergent sibling for not being able to do what was asked. It can lead to self-esteem issues or secondary issues as well if the conflict isn't resolved or ends up being compounded.

Another challenge that your child may face is the communication aspect of being a sibling. Siblings often hold private conversations right out in the open, without anyone around them being the wiser. A lot of this communication is done through the use of a plethora of nonverbal communication and indirect communication such as inside jokes, sarcastic comments, or quiet side eyes—the exact communication techniques that can often cause the most amount of issues for children with autism. For your neurotypical child, this may cause challenges because they'll have to learn that this isn't a part of the relationship they'll likely ever have. They'll still form a unique bond with their sibling, there's no doubt about that, but the way they may have seen siblings depicted in media and expected to have developed is unlikely to happen, which can cause growing frustration for them.

One of the most frustrating aspects that your neurotypical child may run into when it comes to being the sibling of a neurodivergent child, however, is that they will consistently run into places where there may be a double standard. Though conscious effort may be put in to close that gap as much as possible, there's no way to completely eliminate it because your neurodivergent child simply has different needs and will therefore have different rules to adhere to. This will be frustrating for your neurotypical child who may want the same later bedtime, who may want to be able to do their homework in a quiet bedroom rather than at the table where they aren't being observed or may want to be able to wear headphones while eating dinner. The frustration when they're younger will come from being left out. When they're older, the frustration will come from understanding why they're being left out. No matter how understanding your child is, there has to be an understanding that a variation in parenting styles from kid to kid will be irritating and noted, and it will need to be addressed to reduce the amount of friction—but also give your neurotypical children space to vent these frustrations, to validate their feelings, and to give them the ability to have other ways to get benefits that your neurodivergent child might not in an attempt to even the playing field a little.

The Need for Compassion as a Family

As a parent, no matter what diagnoses your child may or may not have, it's understood that a majority of the financial, emotional, and mental support of the family will come from you—and hopefully, that burden is shared with a spouse or reliable co-parent. This is not always the case, however, so building out your own support system can be an important first step before addressing the family unit—a topic that's covered in depth in the following chapter.

With neurodivergent children, however, the load that you need to bear becomes compounded, no matter how severe or mild your child's symptoms may be. Your obligations to your family become split between your neurodivergent child's needs, your spouse, and your neurotypical children. These needs may vary from person to person in your family and cause you to be spread thin.

This is where working as a family unit becomes integral to the success of all parts of your family. Rather than carrying the brunt of the family's needs, make sure to share those responsibilities with any spouses or adults around you that you can. The other part of it, though, is to implement ways for all of the people involved in your family to come together, understand the part they play, and offer understanding for those days when things get difficult.

It is also understood that in places where parents can't be, such as school or sporting events, siblings will stand up for each other—in this case, the neurotypical siblings standing up for their siblings with autism. This doesn't ask of them more than any other sibling in any other relationship would do, but it does extend farther, especially for those kids with autism who might not even understand they're being made fun of or might not know how to defend themselves at all. A sibling to stand up for them in those difficult situations is an excellent addition to the advocacy team. An understanding of autism, however, is important for your neurotypical child to have in order to know that they need to step in and what to say to make sure their sibling feels supported and protected. It can also be the line between knowing when to step in and knowing when to call in a higher authority to deal with a more serious situation such as a physical altercation in a bullying scenario.

Meeting Your Neurotypical Children's Needs

One of the most important aspects of having a neurodivergent child in the family is remembering the other people who are also part of your family unit—in this case, your neurotypical children who also have needs and require attention and affection. It is usually unintentional, but in households where a child has additional needs and requires more involvement than a child who doesn't, the child who doesn't may sometimes get pushed to the wayside since they're interpreted as being able to "fend for themselves." Unfortunately, this can lead to a fracturing of trust, resentment among the family, and even self-esteem issues in your neurotypical child as they may feel less important or less valuable than your neurodivergent children.

This can be especially true for children who have other disorders already present such as depression or anxiety where their self-esteem may already be impacted. My eldest daughter was formally diagnosed with generalized anxiety a few years after my youngest's ASD and ADHD diagnosis, but these symptoms were present all throughout her childhood and especially heightened when her brother was first getting diagnosed with ASD and ADHD and there was a lot of confusion. One of the things my wife and I had to do was make sure that her anxiety wasn't being invalidated or diminished in favor of her younger brother, as neglecting her needs would never be justified in any scenario. It was always important to us that our children's needs were being met in equal amounts—even if they needed to be met in different ways.

To avoid any and all of the above, keep your neurotypical children's needs in mind as much as your neurodivergent child. Though it's understood that they may not always take front and center when there's a crisis with their sibling, make sure that there are times when they do take front and center, when their accomplishments are celebrated, when their wants are being heard and delivered on, and, most importantly, when their needs are being met. Comfort them when they're frustrated—even if that frustration stems from a situation that arose because of you or their sibling—and give them support when they need it. Neurotypical children are also prone to conditions like anxiety, depression, and general illness, so make sure that these are not being ignored or pushed to the back burner for the sake of prioritizing your neurodivergent child's needs or in pursuit of trying to keep your neurodivergent child from catching whatever the virus or infection might be in cases like that.

The Pressure of Expectation

The most crucial part of meeting your neurotypical child's needs, however, is making sure that you're not putting additional pressure on your neurotypical children to fill in the spaces that your neurodivergent child might fall short. This means if your child with autism can't keep up with their chores, it shouldn't be expected of your other children that they take up that responsibility. It also shouldn't be expected of your other children that they are understanding of the situation all the time. Remember that they are also young and they are allowed and valid in expressing their frustrations and feelings when it comes to the challenges of living with someone with autism.

When we place pressure on our other children to fill in the "gaps" left by a child who simply isn't capable of keeping up, it sets the expectation that their worth is only measured by how best they can serve. It also shows them that they're expected to prioritize the needs of the family and their autistic sibling—not themselves. While a certain level of compromise can be understood—at least from older children—to ask your children as a whole to give more of themselves simply because one of their siblings differs from them in some ways isn't fair.

When I explained this to some of the families in some of my community groups, a lot of what I heard back was, "Well, life isn't fair," and "Well, who's supposed to help me around the house, then?"

The answer to the first is: You're right. Life isn't fair. But there's no need for your children to learn that from you or at four years old because they need to wake up to help you deal with their older sibling's meltdown at three in the morning. That is an adult task, something that you as a parent need to handle. Your other children should be allowed to stay children and participate in activities with their siblings that are within the realm of childhood—not adulthood. Sure, they can understand the implications of how autism changes that dynamic, and they may even want to understand how to help out when they can, but it shouldn't be the expectation that they should. Forcing young children to grow up in such a way can be traumatizing and detrimental to them in differing ways and lead to various other issues later in life—a scope of conversation that this book is just not long enough to cover.

The answer to the second question is even more simple: Other adults are supposed to help you, not your young children. There are two givens here that can complicate that—that childcare is expensive, a cost that is only compounded with children who need additional support such as those with autism, and not everyone has a reliable support system to fall back on. To those who fall into the category of both, it becomes a sticky situation. What adults are available to you? I encourage you to look for community groups in your area, support programs, and aid for children with challenging disorders who might need additional aid at home, and to reach out to friends and family for support if you're able to. I also encourage you to read Chapter 8 to learn more about these networking strategies and taking care of yourself. Never, though, will the answer from me ever be to rely on your young children during these times of need.

As an exception to the rule, it may make sense for older children to start playing more of a role in the house. Teenagers can babysit younger children, help to provide care and aid for those who need it when they work late some nights, and might even be able to help in a bigger way when particularly challenging days become catastrophic. Still, there's a limit to how much involvement they should have. At the end of the day, parents should remain in a parenting role while siblings should maintain their role as a sibling.

To Recap

The entire family can be involved in the diagnosis and play a key role in your autistic child's support system—but it's essential that all parts of the team also feel that they're supported and that their needs are being met as well. It can be an overwhelming undertaking to balance everyone in the house, which is why it takes everyone's understanding and cooperation to get everyone on the same page. To do this, everyone must first understand what autism is, what the impacts of the disorder are on the person who has it and everyone around them, and how they can best be involved in the family unit. It's also important to remember that every person is capable of different things, so siblings shouldn't be expected to do more than what their role demands of them, and you as the parent should still be there to make up the majority of the support. The main issue with this, however, is that the support can take its toll. This is where a network for you as the parent comes in handy as well as self-care techniques to make sure not just your family's needs are being met but your own as well.

Chapter 8:

Building a Strong Foundation—Parenting Mindset and Self-Care

A key player in making sure that your children are feeling cared for, supported, and understood the way that they deserve is making sure that you as the parent are feeling cared for, supported, and understood as well. I've already stated in several places throughout the book that even though your child is the one who is diagnosed with, experiencing, and living with their disorder firsthand, you are also handling the challenges that come with their disorder. There's no denying that playing that role for your children is incredibly demanding and can take its toll if it's not properly addressed. That's why it is so important to include a chapter such as this in order to discuss taking care of yourself and making sure that in addition to your children's and spouse's needs, your needs are being met as well.

The Challenges of Parenting a Child With Autism

Though it sounds cruel to state this, the truth of the matter is that children with autism—or any neurodevelopmental disorder for that matter—require more parental involvement and have more demands than children without it. The threat of meltdown, the need to be ready for any changes or challenges that life throws so that you can then prepare your child, and the necessity to always be ready to deal with the quirks of communicating with an autistic child require almost superhuman abilities of patience, focus, and information processing. Being a parent to a neurodivergent child means always being ready to provide support to your child and being ready to provide coping strategies for those situations when they may not be able to express themselves the way that they need to.

Prioritizing your child in this way is almost an expectation from other parents. If you aren't constantly sacrificing yourself, you run the risk of being labeled as a bad parent—which doesn't make any sense at all. The more exhausted you are, the more likely you are to act on impulse and say something off-color to your child. If your needs are being met, you'll be in a better place to pause, process, and respond constructively rather than lashing out—because it needs to be understood that even adults can have bad days too, and especially parents.

Social pressure is something that we can never escape even into parenthood and it can lead us to make poor decisions even when we know what's best for us. That pressure from other parents can be enough to keep you from doing what you need to to keep yourself happy and healthy. This will lead to you doing whatever you can for your children and neglecting those moments when you should be doing something for yourself.

This may seem like a small and unimportant detail to you. It may even seem selfish to consider yourself when your child struggles with the stigma and challenges that come with living with a disorder like autism. It's important to remember for yourself, though, that you're also there with them during every part of that—supporting them and advocating for them, working with them through those meltdowns, and learning everything you can about their disorder as a front-line of defense against those that try to dismiss them. That leaves you in the thick of it as much as you can be without having been diagnosed yourself. You're also in charge of managing, maintaining, and censoring your own emotions even during the most challenging of those days so as to not set them off and to offer them all the love and support that you can even when they may not be able to return it. This constant need to be at the ready can quickly lead to a sense of burnout—which can segue quickly into a sense of guilt.

I mentioned this in my first book but it needs to be mentioned again here for everyone's sanity: You are not the first and you will not be the last person to experience burnout as a parent. You also have no reason to feel guilty for experiencing it. When you overextend yourself like this for a long period of time, the only logical conclusion would be to reach—or even exceed—your limits. We have finite energy as humans, and even if we want to convince ourselves that we can keep going, it just simply isn't possible to continue to push through once that limit is hit.

Understanding where your limits are is a very important factor in avoiding burnout, or at the very least minimizing it. The other components would be using the resources available to you, building a strong support system, or building times into your routine for you to step away and regroup even when you're on your own. Even small amounts of time can make a huge difference.

Before learning how to deal with burnout and knowing who to involve in the process of bearing the burden, however, you need to first understand exactly what burnout is, the guilt that it brings, and how it can affect you.

Burnout and Guilt

Burnout is the result of doing too much for too long without stopping, or pushing yourself beyond your limits repeatedly and ignoring your body's need to stop and rest. It can occur for many reasons, such as working multiple jobs, going to school, and participating in sports at the same time, and, of course, parenting children—particularly parenting children who require additional need and care. Along with this last one usually comes a heaping serving of guilt because parents often feel like they're blaming their child or like they're failing their child for not being able to handle the stresses of parenthood.

Burnout comes in different stages, and usually begins with exhaustion and ends with an inability to do what's asked of you as a parent (CHADD, 2023). This could mean that you're not able to care for your child effectively or meet their needs—even without meaning to—simply because the task becomes too overwhelming or exhausting for you to be able to handle and complete effectively. Burnout may also lead you to stop promoting positive parenting behavior in favor of less desirable tactics to try to minimize the demand on yourself—which can lead to a negative home environment for your child and can cause more issues than it's worth (CHADD, 2023).

Guilt is also a major factor in burnout, part of this vicious cycle of feeling guilty for doing the wrong thing but not having the energy to right it and being pushed further into this void by feeling like you're a bad parent anyway. While I can't particularly absolve you of that guilt, I can tell you that you're not alone. Even as parents of neurodivergent children, we're not alone. Parental guilt is a parent-wide experience. My friends with neurotypical kids also feel guilty for parenting mistakes they've made. We all make mistakes. We all feel like we're doing it wrong.

Where the challenge for us here comes in is that we feel we shouldn't be exhausted by our children—and I'm also here to tell you that this is also entirely natural. Being a parent is an exhausting job. It isn't easy—in fact, it's overly complicated—and there are so many rules with so many exceptions that you'll think you have it down only for the rules to change again. The only right way, in truth, is the way that keeps your kid happy and healthy, keeps your head on your shoulders, and raises a decent human being. This is a key part of being able to forgive yourself. So long as you are doing your best by way of your child and doing what you can to make sure they're the best they can be, then you're doing fine.

In the context of your burnout, understand that exhaustion is part of parenting. The key to avoiding this guilt and this bone tiredness and sometimes hopelessness is to set yourself up for success by making sure that your needs are being met in addition to theirs.

Coping With It

A lot of these techniques will be the same as in the first book, as even though this one discusses a different disorder, many of the coping skills for parents will remain the same. This is because, as with most things, self-care starts with a few basic things. Though it can end up evolving into different forms or different activities, where those activities begin will almost always start at the same place—a place that works. So, at the risk of sounding repetitive, here are some things to consider to help you avoid or cope with the burnout of parenting a child with a neurodevelopmental disorder like autism.

Mindfulness

Mindfulness is often confused with meditation, and while meditation can play a factor in the activity, it doesn't make up the whole part of it. In its simplest definition, mindfulness means to be present with yourself and check in with your own needs and demands so you can make somewhat of a mental catalog of where your mind and body are at and adjust accordingly.

Meditation

Because it was mentioned, explaining meditation first might be beneficial just to explain the role that it can play in mindfulness and self-care. For a lot of people, meditation can feel like a weighted task because it can be time-consuming, involves a lot of silence, and demands a lot of focus on the self. For many people, any one of these things can feel uncomfortable or might be hard to achieve. Time alone to mediate might be too much to ask for when it comes to trying to manage a household for some. Yet meditating for as short as even five minutes in the morning has been shown to help set a calmer pace for the day. Waking up before the rest of the family can be a good time to do this. It can also be more than just sitting and letting your mind wander. It can be an intentional meditation like a mantra repeating ceremony or even a body check-in.

Body Scans

Body scans are one useful tool when it comes to mindfulness because they can be done anywhere and they don't take a lot of time to do. When doing a body scan, simply take a couple of deep breaths and introspectively evaluate the different areas of your body. While doing these, you can assess what you feel in different areas of your body and try to correct it. For instance, you may notice that your shoulders might be tense, that your stomach might be tight, or that your jaw might be clenched. While doing the body scan, you can take the time to relax these parts of your body to try to give yourself a moment of relief.

Breathing Exercises

Breathing exercises can also be a simple and easy way to regulate at the moment when time isn't on your side. Deep breaths and 360 breathing can help to bring a sense of calm to your body and can help to stimulate the vagus nerve which plays a big part in the mind-body connection, meaning it can be a big source of tension for the body. By breathing and stimulating that main nerve, it can help to release a lot of tension that may be held in the stomach and in smaller areas throughout the rest of the body as well. It may also help to stimulate a larger release in times when emotions may be hard to reach—such as crying or screaming when you have time for that. Though it may seem silly, screaming and crying in a big burst can help in a cathartic way and truly lead to a more positive feeling on the other side.

Self-Care Practices

This is such a broad statement because self-care looks different for every person and because "self-care" doesn't have a distinct definition. For some, self-care is as simple as screaming into a pillow to let it out. For others, it's a hot bath with a glass of wine and a good book. For others still, it's chopping wood in the backyard to blow off some steam. Everyone's self-care is different—but at the core of it are two things: destressing and meeting your needs in the best way you can.

Some of the simplest ways to help yourself feel better are to take part in things that you enjoy—be it the wood chopping mentioned above, crocheting on the couch while the kids watch TV, or even coloring a coloring book at the kitchen table while your kids color their own books in the living room. For some, and especially for my wife, the best way for her to destress is to take a really hot, really long shower. She doesn't like baths, but having the water run over her head from top to toes helps her to feel like the stress is truly running off of her body, and it can turn her mood around just like that. She can go into the shower on the verge of tears and come out refreshed and ready to take on anything that's thrown at her.

The point of including this is to remind you that self-care is not just doing the things you see on self-care blogs like using diffusers, lighting candles, participating in mindfulness, and using elaborate hygiene routines to take care of your external body. It's also participating in hobbies that bring you joy and doing things that make you happy to bring you care on the inside as well. Taking care of your happiness is just as important, at least in my opinion as someone in the same position as you, as brushing your teeth.

Managing Expectations

Just as you do with your neurotypical children in your household environment by not expecting more of them than you should, remember to also reflect this back on yourself. You are only one person, only capable of so much at one time, and you should be understanding and compassionate of your own limitations. Be realistic when it comes to the amount that you can handle in one day and be kind to yourself when things go slightly off the rails. Nothing will ever go exactly according to plan, but so long as the kids are happy and fed, you are happy and fed, and everyone's needs are being met and supported, then you've done your job. Don't expect to be able to do everything all the time. Praise your successes, forgive your failures, and understand your limitations so you're always in a positive mindset.

Setting Your Own Routines

Having routines that are separate from your child's can also be a major game changer when it comes to fighting burnout. While most parents' lives are dictated by their child's schedule, and no schedule is more dictated than that of a child with a neurodevelopmental disorder like autism, building in set times for yourself to be an adult, to take care of your needs, and to get your own tasks done can be the difference between continuous overwhelm and being on top of your game—or at least having a handle on it.

Since your child already has a pretty structured routine to help manage their symptoms and needs, it can be easier to implement your own schedule and needs around that. Getting up before them in the morning to drink your coffee, to meditate if you feel that would be helpful, or to do something that brings you joy can be a good way to give you peace of mind before the chaos of the day begins. Having a set routine of what happens every morning can also be helpful so you know nothing's been forgotten, that all your children are accounted for, and that each task for the day has its time and place. Alternatively, you could schedule extra time in the evening that is just for you, when the kids go off to play and you aren't doing chores, but just doing something entirely for yourself.

It can also be important to schedule time during the week—such as a larger block on the weekend or perhaps one night a week—where you're able to get an extended period away to do something fun or to get tasks done that have been looming over your head without interruption. This is when it can be useful to tag in childcare, trusted family members or friends, or hopefully rely on a partner to split the childcare responsibility while you tend to the other needs of adult life. Taking time away from the children doesn't make you a bad parent. In the long run, it could even make you a better one as you'll be more centered, you'll not be worried about half a dozen things at once, and you'll have a happier center.

Forming a Network

Important People

If it is possible to you, the best place to start is with close friends and family members, who will be most likely to have both your and your child's best interests at heart. Though not all family units are like this, if you do have one as such, it can be the best and most beneficial arrangement. Before all else, though, your spouse or co-parent is the number one person to turn to for additional support while raising a neurodivergent child.

Having doctors and other professionals like counselors and therapists who are intricately familiar with your child's case are also good people to have in mind when it comes to your support system. This way, when things get tough for your child or require additional intervention, you have a team of supportive people you can call and you know exactly when and how to contact them and understand that they'll know exactly how to best help your child. Though they are there predominantly for your child, knowing that they'll have their best interest in mind takes the pressure off you and will ease your worry—as much as one can ease the worry of a parent—and it can take some of the panic from you.

School teachers and aids are also an important part of your own support system, as they are your direct line to what your child is doing and how they are succeeding in school. Knowing that your child is being supported and understood in school is another great way to help distribute the burden of worry.

A lot of the above does rely on the fact that you have people in your corner, however, as previously mentioned, it can't be assumed that everyone does. The good news is that there are now a lot of resources for those looking for a support system for children with disabilities. Community support groups, where I started, are a great place to meet others looking for the same kind of support as you. I found an abundance of other families who were in the same boat as me, and it helped more than I realized just to be able to commiserate with others about my experiences with my son. Simply knowing that I wasn't alone and that my son wasn't alone kept a sense of positivity in those early days when I was trying to wrap my head around what his diagnoses meant. I became good friends with some of those folks, too, and over the years, we've watched each other's children and shared contacts for babysitters who did well with our kids.

To Recap

Caring for children as a whole is a stressful and taxing task. Caring for children with autism can be even more difficult at times because of the continuous demand to advocate for them and make sure that they're being cared for and protected in a world that refuses to accept them for who they are. But when you are not functioning at your best, then you can not do your best for your children. This means that it's incredibly important that you take care of yourself as much as you take care of those around you to ensure that you are putting out the best of yourself for both your sake and theirs. Time to reflect internally, to do things that you enjoy, and to provide yourself peace are important when it comes to being a parent. It's also important to know how much you can realistically do in a day and to understand that when you don't meet your expectations, it is probably because they were too high. Parenting is all about grace and forgiveness—for your children and for yourself.

A lot of self-care comes from having the right people around you to support you so that you're able to help your kids the way that they need. Family members, friends, medical professionals, teachers, and other parents experiencing the same things that you are are all an important part of this support network which can help you to avoid burnout and to remind you to take care of yourself when things get a little hairy. They can also help you forgive yourself when parent guilt sets in and provide you a little extra peace of mind in knowing that your child has an entire village behind them, not just you, and that you have an entire village too.

Conclusion

Autism spectrum disorder is a complicated thing. It's often steeped in ridicule and stigma due to the continued myths and misunderstandings that surround it, even from people who live with those who have the disorder. Children with ASD are believed to be cold, distant, and sometimes violent because of their inability to interact with the world in the way that people expect them to. In reality, ASD is treated the way it is simply because of misunderstandings and myths that have led to a distortion of what it really is. This lack of understanding is also why an autism diagnosis can seem so disappointing and dooming. Without a firm grasp of what the disorder is, these stigmas can be inadvertently perpetuated by the parents of children with autism and lead to strenuous family relationships and low self-esteem in those who have been diagnosed.

What makes disorders like autism easier to stomach is that it isn't a rare disorder to encounter and there are a lot of resources out there to help you understand what you'll be up against. Even with each experience being different from person to person, there is so much overlap between symptoms that no matter what you run into with your child, someone will understand what your child is going through—and you as their parent—and be able to offer some insights. The most important part of all of it is to first understand what your child has so that you know what you're looking for. This is why early diagnosis and intervention can be so vital to the development of a child with autism. Misdiagnoses and mistreatment can often lead to a delay in the necessary aid that children with autism need.

Once you have a diagnosis, that's where the true work starts though. Resources that help you explain what autism really is are key players in making sure you find what you're looking for when it comes to aid. That was one of the main goals of this book, to help give a real-life explanation of what autism is as well as techniques that I've tried with my son or families that I've known have tried to help their child cope with their disorder. This way, you'll have a place to start when it comes to getting your child the help they need by way of understanding, coping with, and thriving with their symptoms.

The most important thing to take away from this is that autism is a disorder of communication, meaning that your child will never find a place where they truly are without conflict. When dialogue is required, when body language and tone are playing a factor, or when information needs to be filtered through and processed, there will always be more asked of your child than they may be able or willing to participate in which will put them at a constant disadvantage. There are ways to help them though. As a parent, it's your job to help them understand how to use whatever communication skills they can to help dictate what's happening inside their head. It's not simple, but through trial and error, it can be figured out. By practicing communication, giving them a space at home to communicate in a way that benefits them, or providing them with a way to express themselves uniquely, they can find ways to promote their own communication skills without constantly being on edge. They may also struggle with meltdowns due to overstimulation, struggle with peer relationships due to a lack of understanding of social conventions, and have a hard time without structure or routine.

These things can be managed however with the right amount of practice, coping skills, and support from you as the parent. Rewarding them for the good and helping them through the bad can help them understand what good behavior and positive communication look like and what "bad" behavior and negative communication look like. You also want them to know that no matter what they're saying—whether it be a monologue they've given a dozen times about their favorite animal or a question you ask them by way of an answer for something they want—they're being heard as well as understood. Regardless of their communication style, so long as they're doing it effectively, constructively, and you know what they mean, that is truly all that matters. Advocating for this support in schools through IEPs and supportive aids is also a big part of making sure your child feels like they're getting the support they need in all areas of their life.

All of this can only be done, of course, if you're at the top of your game—as we saw in Chapter 8—and if the family is doing everything they can to support one another too—as we saw in Chapter 7. Make sure that your own network is strong, that the family has time to take care of themselves as well as each other, and that there's a little extra compassion for when bad days are happening to all of you. Having bad days is a part of life, and condemning someone for having one won't make it better. Giving grace for those moments can go a lot farther than saying there's no time for them. The important thing is that everyone is provided the time to remember to breathe and that they all know that they are loved.

Autism diagnoses can be overwhelming, but being prepared for what that means can take a lot of that weight away. By reading books like this, getting involved in support groups and community groups for families with autistic children, and listening to your child's needs, you're doing more to get prepared than most. With that knowledge in your wheelhouse, you'll have yourself—and your child—set up for success in no time.

References

American Psychiatric Association. (n.d.). *What is autism spectrum disorder?* https://www.psychiatry.org/patients-families/autism/what-is-autism-spectrum-disorder

The Australian Parenting Website. (2020, November 18). *Challenging behavior: Autistic children and teenagers.* raisingchildren.net.au. https://raisingchildren.net.au/autism/behaviour/understanding-behaviour/challenging-behaviour-asd

Autism Empowerment. (n.d.). *Coexisting conditions.* https://www.autismempowerment.org/understanding-autism/co-existing-conditions/

Autism myths and misconceptions. (n.d.). https://adsd.nv.gov/uploadedFiles/adsdnvgov/content/Programs/Autism/ATAP/Autism%20Myths%20and%20Misconceptions.pdf

Autistica. (2018, April 9). *Autism myths and causes.* https://www.autistica.org.uk/what-is-autism/autism-myths-and-causes

Autistica. (2023, February 26). *Alexithymia.* https://www.autistica.org.uk/what-is-autism/anxiety-and-autism-hub/alexithymia

Bailey, E. (2021, February 3). Is an IEP or 504 plan best for your child? How to decide. *ADDitude.* https://www.additudemag.com/iep-step-5-evaluate-your-options/

Center for Parent Information and Resources. (n.d.). *Transition to adulthood.* https://parentcenterhub.org/transitionadult/

Centers for Disease Control and Prevention. (2022-a, January 25). *Autism and vaccines.* https://www.cdc.gov/vaccinesafety/concerns/autism.html

Centers for Disease Control and Prevention. (2022-b, March 31). *Screening and diagnosis.* https://www.cdc.gov/ncbddd/autism/screening.html

Centers for Disease Control and Prevention. (2022-c, December 9). *ASD diagnosis, treatment, and services.* https://www.cdc.gov/ncbddd/autism/facts.html

Centers for Disease Control and Prevention. (2023, January 11). *Signs and symptoms of autism spectrum disorder.* https://www.cdc.gov/ncbddd/autism/signs.htm

Children and Adults with Attention-Deficit/Hyperactivity Disorder. (2018, May 8). *Build self-esteem in your child with ADHD.* https://chadd.org/adhd-weekly/build-self-esteem-in-your-child-with-adhd/

Children and Adults with Attention-Deficit/Hyperactivity Disorder. (2023, July 20). *Irritable and overwhelmed? Signs of parental burnout.* https://chadd.org/adhd-news/adhd-news-caregivers/irritable-and-overwhelmed-signs-of-parental-burnout/

Cleveland Clinic. (2022-a, June 15). *Dysgraphia.* https://my.clevelandclinic.org/health/diseases/23294-dysgraphia

Cleveland Clinic. (2022-b, August 2). *Dyscalculia.* https://my.clevelandclinic.org/health/diseases/23949-dyscalculia

Dale, J. (2022, March 5). *How to improve communication with people with autism.* Calvert Exmoor. https://calvertexmoor.org.uk/news/improve-communication-with-autistic-people/

Edelson, S. (2022, June 16). Understanding challenging behaviors in autism spectrum disorder: A multi-component, interdisciplinary model. *Journal of Personalized Medicine, 12*(7), 1127. 10.3390/jpm12071127.

Eunice Kennedy Shriver National Institute of Child Health and Human Development. (2017, January 31). *What causes autism?* National Institute of Health. https://www.nichd.nih.gov/health/topics/autism/conditioninfo/causes

Gehret, M. (2020, August 6). *Autism and learning disabilities.* Spectrum of Hope. https://spectrumofhope.com/blog/autism-and-learning-disorders/

Lee, A. M. I. (2020, October 22). *When a child with an IEP turns 18: Your parental rights.* Understood. https://www.understood.org/en/articles/when-your-child-with-an-iep-turns-18-your-parental-rights

Lindor, E., Sivaratnam, C., May, T., Stefanac, N., Howells, K., & Rinehart, N. (2019, July 12). Problem behavior in autism spectrum disorder: Considering core symptom severity and accompanying sleep disturbance. *Frontiers Psychiatry, 10,* 487. https://doi.org/10.3389/fpsyt.2019.00487

Marcus Autism Center. (n.d.). *Tackling problem behaviors.* Children's Healthcare of Atlanta. https://www.marcus.org/autism-resources/autism-tips-and-resources/tackling-problem-behaviors

Margolis, A. E., Broitman, J., Davis, J. M., Alexander, L., Hamilton, A., Liao, Z., Banker, S., Thomas, L., Ramphal, B., Salum, G. A., Merikangas, K., Goldsmith, J., Paus, T., Keyes, K., & Milham, M. P. (2020, April). Estimated prevalence of nonverbal learning disability among North American children and adolescents. *JAMA network open, 3*(4), e202551. https://doi.org/10.1001/jamanetworkopen.2020.2551

Marner, K. (2022, March 31). Real IEP accommodations that really work. *ADDitude.* https://www.additudemag.com/iep-accommodations-what-works-for-us/

Massachusetts Department of Elementary and Secondary Education. (2015, March 12). *Transition from school to adult life.* https://www.doe.mass.edu/sped/links/transition.html

Mayo Clinic. (2022, August 6). *Dyslexia.* https://www.mayoclinic.org/diseases-conditions/dyslexia/symptoms-causes/syc-20353552

McKinney, J. (2021, October 7). *Life after the IEP: How do I help my child with a disability transition to adulthood?* Exceptional Lives. https://exceptionallives.org/blog/life-after-the-iep-how-do-i-help-my-child-with-a-disability-transition-to-adulthood/

Miller, C. (2023, July 13). *What is non-verbal learning disorder?* Child Mind Institute. https://childmind.org/article/what-is-non-verbal-learning-disorder/

Morin, A. (2022, November 2). *How to create a token system to improve your child's behavior.* VeryWell Family. https://www.verywellfamily.com/create-a-token-economy-system-to-improve-child-behavior-1094888

Morin, A. (2023-b, June 15). *The difference between discipline and punishment.* Understood.

Morin, A. (2023-b, June 15). *Parenting guilt: Tips to get past it.* Understood. https://www.understood.org/en/articles/parent-guilt-tips

https://www.understood.org/articles/the-difference-between-discipline-and-punishment

Mosner, M. G., Kinard, J. L., Shah, J. S., McWeeny, S., Greene, R. K., Lowery, S. C., Mazefsky, C. A., & Dichter, G. S. (2019). Rates of co-occurring psychiatric disorders in autism spectrum disorder using the mini international neuropsychiatric interview. *Journal of Autism and Developmental Disorders, 49*(9), 3819-3832. https://doi.org/10.1007/s10803-019-04090-1

National Autistic Society. (2020, August 20). *Communication tips.* https://www.autism.org.uk/advice-and-guidance/topics/communication/tips

National Institute on Deafness and Other Communication Disorders. (2020, April 13). *Autism spectrum disorder: Communication problems in children.* National Institute of Health. https://www.nidcd.nih.gov/health/autism-spectrum-disorder-communication-problems-children

National Institute of Mental Health. (2023, February). *Autism spectrum disorder.* https://www.nimh.nih.gov/health/topics/autism-spectrum-disorders-asd

National University. (2023, August 18). *7 autism behavior and communication strategies.* https://www.nu.edu/blog/7-autism-behavior-and-communication-strategies/

Nerney, J. (2021, May 18). 4 self care tips for parents of kids with ADHD. RevibeTech. https://blog.revibetech.com/4-self-care-tips-for-parents-of-kids-with-adhd

News Medical Life Sciences. (2020, April 28). *Study: Nonverbal learning disability is more common than believed.* News Medical. https://www.news-medical.net/news/20200428/Study-Nonverbal-learning-disability-is-more-common-than-believed.aspx

NHS Fife. (2023, February 9). *Autism spectrum disorder (ASD).* NHS Inform. https://www.nhsinform.scot/illnesses-and-conditions/brain-nerves-and-spinal-cord/autism-spectrum-disorder-asd

Nicole. (2022, January, 5). *Challenging behaviors and autism.* Autism Research Institute. https://autism.org/challenging-behaviors-and-autism/

Novak, S. (2022, December 7). *Autism myths and facts.* WebMD. https://www.webmd.com/brain/autism/features/autism-myths-facts

Paavolva, A. (2022, October 6). *Tone indicators: A master list, what they are, and how to use them.* Textline. https://www.textline.com/blog/tone-indicator-list

Powell, B. T. (2023). *Raising champions: A roadmap to success in ADHD parenting.* Independently Published.

Rodden, J. (2023, January 21). What is autism spectrum disorder? *ADDitude.* https://www.additudemag.com/what-is-autism-spectrum-disorder-asd/

The Spectrum. (2020, February 13). *Autism communication strategies.* https://thespectrum.org.au/autism-strategy/autism-strategy-communication/

SSM Health. (n.d.). *Savant syndrome.* https://www.ssmhealth.com/treffert-center/conditions-treatments/savant-syndrome

University of Rochester Medical Center. (n.d.). *Interacting with a child who has autism spectrum disorder.* https://www.urmc.rochester.edu/encyclopedia/content.aspx?contenttypeid=160&contentid=46

Wakeling, R. (2020, November 19). *How to develop self confidence in children on the autism spectrum.* The Spectrum. https://thespectrum.org.au/how-to-develop-self-confidence-in-children-on-the-autism-spectrum/

Wilkinson, L. A. (2017, March 1). *Alexithymia, empathy, and autism.* Living Autism. https://livingautism.com/alexithymia-empathy-autism/

Milton Keynes UK
Ingram Content Group UK Ltd.
UKHW020237221123
432980UK00016B/1201